I0797782

# THE ARCHITECTURE OF THE PLAYING FIELD

Terry and Jan Todd Series on Physical Culture and Sports
Edited by Sarah K. Fields, Thomas Hunt, Daniel A. Nathan, and Patricia Vertinsky

ALSO IN THE SERIES

Maureen M. Smith, Daniel A. Nathan, and Sarah K. Fields, eds., *Sports through the Lens: Essays on 25 Iconic Photographs*

Jonathan Silverman, editor, *Astros and Asterisks: Houston's Sign-Stealing Scandal Explained*

Adam Berg, *The Olympics That Never Happened: Denver '76 and the Politics of Growth*

Michella M. Marino, *Roller Derby: The History of an American Sport*

Ronald A. Smith, *The Myth of the Amateur: A History of College Athletic Scholarships*

Andrew R. M. Smith, *No Way but to Fight: George Foreman and the Business of Boxing*

Jason P. Shurley, Jan Todd, and Terry Todd, *Strength Coaching in America: A History of the Innovation That Transformed Sports*

Kevin Robbins, *Harvey Penick: The Life and Wisdom of the Man Who Wrote the Book on Golf*

John Hoberman, *Dopers in Uniform: The Hidden World of Police on Steroids*

John D. Fair, *Mr. America: The Tragic History of a Bodybuilding Icon*

Thomas M. Hunt, *Drug Games: The International Olympic Committee and the Politics of Doping, 1960–2008*

# THE ARCHITECTURE OF THE PLAYING FIELD

## SHAPING SPACE IN SPORT

RICHARD L. CLEARY

University of Texas Press *Austin*

Printed in the United States of America
First edition, 2025



♾ The paper used in this book meets the minimum requirements of ANSI/NISO Z39.48–1992 (R1997) (Permanence of Paper).

Cataloging-in-Publication Data is available from the Library of Congress.

ISBN 978–1-4773-3129-3 (cloth)
ISBN 978–1-4773-3130-9 (PDF)
ISBN 978–1-4773-3131-6 (ePub)

doi:10.7560/331293

# CONTENTS

*List of Illustrations* vi

*Introduction* 1

CHAPTER 1. **FRAMES** 15

CHAPTER 2. **MEDIATED SPACE** 47

CHAPTER 3. **LABORATORIES OF SPATIAL INVENTION** 77

CHAPTER 4. **SPORTS, SPACE, AND CULTURE** 107

EPILOGUE. **BIG AIR** 127

*Acknowledgments* 139

*Notes* 141

*Bibliography* 158

*Index* 170

# ILLUSTRATIONS


Figure 0.1. Eduardo Chillida, *Elogio del Horizonte* *7*

Figure 0.2. Kazimir Malevich, *Painterly Realism of a Football Player—Color Masses in the 4th Dimension* *8*

Figure 0.3. Tennis players. Le Corbusier, *The City of Tomorrow and Its Planning* *9*

Figure 0.4. CopenHill, Copenhagen *10*

Figure 1.1. PSA Women's Squash World Championship, Giza, Egypt, 2019 *16*

Figure 1.2. St. Peter's Park, Ashton, Wisconsin *18*

Figure 1.3. Women's Épée Individual competition, London 2012 Summer Olympics *19*

Figure 1.4. PNC Park, Pittsburgh *21*

Figure 1.5. Baseball strike zone *25*

Figure 1.6. Soccer pitch, Mühlheim an der Ruhr, Germany *28*

Figure 1.7. Syracuse University stadium, Syracuse, New York, 1910 *30*

Figure 1.8. Squash court *32*

Figure 1.9. University of Wisconsin–Madison freshman women's basketball team, 1900 *35*

Figure 1.10. Adidas Arena, Porte de La Chapelle, Paris *37*

Figure 1.11. Erin Hills Golf Course, Erin, Wisconsin *40*

Figure 1.12. 16th hole, Cypress Point golf course, Pebble Beach, California *43*

Figure 2.1. Listeners' guide to the Crystal Palace Football Ground, 1927 *51*
Figure 2.2. Kinescope recording screenshot, 1952 World Series *56*
Figure 2.3. One-handed touchdown catch by Odell Beckham Jr., 2014 *62*
Figure 2.4. Andy Murray watches a Hawk-Eye electronic line call, Wimbledon Championships, 2015 *72*
Figure 3.1. New Zealand Black Ferns perform a *haka,* 2021 Women's Rugby League World Cup, before their match vs. Australia Wallaroos *78*
Figure 3.2. Combined figure skating, *Figure Skating Simple and Combined* *81*
Figure 3.3. "Football at the Oval—England v. Scotland," 1879 *84*
Figure 3.4. "The Original Flying Wedge, Harvard's famous formation about to attack Yale," 1892 *86*
Figure 3.5. Mesh play *87*
Figure 3.6. Jake Barnett, St. Louis University, shoots from the corner, 2013 *89*
Figure 3.7. Swimmers in an Olympic-size pool *98*
Figure 4.1. The former site of Ayresome Park, Middlesbrough, UK, with Neville Gabie's installation *The Trophy Room* *110*
Figure 4.2. Grand Sumo at the Fukuoka Kokusai Center, Fukuoka, Japan, 2009 *113*
Figure 4.3. Ryōgoku Kokugikan, Tokyo, 1909 *114*
Figure 4.4. Lacrosse match, Montréal club vs. Mohawks of Kahnawà:ke, 1870 *120*
Figure 4.5. Johan Ferner Ström, *Puckelboll,* interactive art installation, Malmö, Sweden *123*
Figure 5.1. Kaishu Hirano, Men's Halfpipe Final, Beijing 2022 Winter Olympics *128*

Figure 5.2. Queralt Castellet, Chloe Kim, and Sena Tomita, Women's Halfpipe medalists, Beijing 2022 Winter Olympics *132*

Figure 5.3. Composite image showing Shaun White executing a backside double McTwist 1260, PyeongChang 2018 Winter Olympics *135*

# THE ARCHITECTURE OF THE PLAYING FIELD

# INTRODUCTION

Gazing at the landscape passing beneath the airplane window on an evening flight, my eyes are drawn to the glowing rectangles, ovals, and diamonds of lighted sports fields. Sometimes, a soccer, football, or baseball game will be in progress, and, for a few moments, I can follow the flow of play: a striker taking a shot on goal, receivers running pass routes, the synchronized movement of infielders making a double play. Most of these scenes occur on recreational fields where players outnumber spectators scattered along the sidelines—family members and faithful friends, perhaps—but on a Friday evening in the fall, I may glimpse the high school stadium of a small town packed with a substantial percentage of the local population wearing the colors of the home team. On a few occasions when I lived in Austin, Texas, my flights home passed above Darrell K Royal–Texas Memorial Stadium during University of Texas at Austin home football games with a hundred thousand burnt-orange-wearing fans in the stands. Although I was far removed from the sounds, bustle, and visual detail of the action, the patterns of play stood out, and I'd try to discern whether the Longhorns were the masters of their turf.

There are many reasons why people enjoy playing and watching sports. Familiar attractions include the exhilaration of vigorous exercise and the pursuit of athletic excellence, the dramatic tension of competition (sometimes heightened by friendly wagers on the outcome), and the camaraderie of teammates and fellow fans. At a more fundamental level, the neuroscientist John Krakauer suggests that sports are an expression of an inherent human predilection as "complexity makers and complexity detectors."[1] Whether a playground pickup game or a professional championship showcased in a monumental stadium, sporting events exercise this predilection.

"Playing a game," writes the philosopher of sport Bernard Suits, "is the voluntary attempt to overcome unnecessary obstacles."[2] In soccer, such an unnecessary obstacle is the proscription of the use of hands or arms to carry or direct the ball by players other than the goalkeepers. In golf, it includes the requirement to use a club to convey a small ball to a hole hundreds of yards away. Acceptance of such challenges sets a game apart from mundane pursuits for which the solution to getting a golf ball to the hole would be simply to pick it up and carry it. Besides regulating actions, voluntary restrictions in sports can address time. The duration of a soccer game, for example, is governed by the relentless count on the ninety-minute clock. Completion of a baseball game, in contrast, depends not on a clock but on the passage of outs and innings. In theory, a baseball game locked in a tied score might never end (some spectators might argue that they have sat through such games). The philosopher of sport R. Scott Kretchmar broadly distinguishes sports governed by events ("E games")—a hole in golf, innings in baseball, reaching the finish line—from those governed by time ("T games")—soccer or basketball, for instance.[3]

Sports also involve the creation of special architectural configurations that establish boundaries and constrain movement in accordance with a game's objectives. When I mention my interest in sports and architecture to friends and casual acquaintances, they understandably think first of stadiums and arenas. This is a subject that in recent years has received increasingly nuanced scholarly attention.[4] My focus, however, is the architecture of the playing fields on which sporting events are contested. Their diversity is remarkable, ranging from the barely discernible course of a sailing race demarcated by a few widely spaced buoys to the sculpted terrain of a golf course to the rigid gridiron of an American football field. This architecture is integral to the structured complexity of sports. It frames possibilities for play, much as floors, walls, ceilings, and stairs frame possibilities for inhabiting a building. Athletes vie to master the spatial constraints of these settings through strategic intent (illustrated by the Xs and Os drawn on a coach's whiteboard) and performance—physical strength, agility, and the cat-and-mouse games of feints intended to confuse their opponents' spatial perception.

The architecture of playing fields frames sporting events as something apart from other pursuits. Reflecting on the properties of frames in general—picture frames, window frames, and the like—the author Karl Ove Knausgaard writes, "The frame limits a phenomenon, sharply demarcates an inside and an outside, and by isolating it, the phenomenon becomes clearly defined, that is it becomes something in itself. It gains an identity. Identity is being one thing and not the other."[5] The simple act of laying out water bottles and backpacks on open ground in a public park to demarcate goals and boundaries for a pickup soccer game frames the undifferentiated space as a soccer pitch.

The actions of players on the field can also be architectural. Radio listeners or television viewers of soccer, American football, basketball, and other sports involving the invasion of an opponent's territory are familiar with play-by-play commentators speaking of players "finding space," "making space," and being "in space." The phrases typically refer to situations in which an attacking player has achieved separation from defenders and obtained an advantageous position to receive a pass, make a run downfield, or take an open shot on goal. While these expressions often are overused to the point of cliché, they capture the competitive challenges of players vying to control the playing field by mentally outwitting and physically overwhelming the opposing efforts of their rivals. Other examples of architectural constructions on the playing field include the "wall" soccer players form to defend a penalty kick by obscuring the most direct trajectory to the goal, the pockets that offensive linemen in American football form to protect the quarterback from pass rushers, and the screens basketball players set to open space for a teammate to drive to the basket or take a shot.

It's a choreography like that of dancers using their bodies to give spatial definition to a bare stage and the occupants of a building responding to the cues for movement and repose devised by the architect. The spatial practices of sports, dance, and architecture appeal to our predilection for complexity in similar ways.

My path to this assertion has wound through all these disciplines. During my high school and college years, I worked behind the scenes with ballet and modern dance companies. Before I knew how to talk about what I was watching from my vantage points in the wings and lighting booths, I was struck by the way the movements of even a solo dancer could shape my perception of space and time. As my understanding of the dancer's craft improved, I came to recognize how choreographers employed repetition to impress spatial patterns in the memories of the audience, much as athletes condition their opponents' expectations before breaking the pattern with a surprise move.

When the study of architectural history took over my life, I absorbed axioms such as the architect Louis Kahn's statement "Architecture is the thoughtful making of spaces," and I became fluent in the architect-speak of space as something that can be bounded, compressed, and made to flow by arrangements of building components.[6] While I appreciate the representation of architecture with photographs, drawings, and models, I am most engaged when I experience buildings directly. Writing in 1914, the critic Geoffrey Scott declared in his influential book *The Architecture of Humanism: A Study in the History of Taste* that spatial experience is at the heart of architectural art: "Space . . . is liberty of movement. That is its value to us, and as such it enters our physical consciousness." The fundamental humanism of architecture for Scott is not the abstraction of space in photographs and drawings but our empathetic, bodily response to architectural forms—arches, colonnades, domes—and how "we have transcribed ourselves into terms of architecture" and "transcribe architecture into terms of ourselves."[7] Many decades later, at the end of the century, the architect Bernard Tschumi highlighted the importance of "activating space through the movement of bodies."[8] In a complementary statement referring to architecture and landscape architecture, the philosopher Arnold Berleant writes, "*We* are the performers in the art of environment."[9] An important aspect of our engagement with buildings and landscapes is the reciprocal transcription of body and architecture that Scott had in mind. The risers, treads, and landings of a staircase, the architect Robert J. Yudell reminds us in his essay "Body Movement," invite physical responses—to step up or down, to pause, to hurry on—based on how we process what we see, our muscle memory of climbing stairs, and our attraction to their inherent complexity.[10] "Architecture," the architectural historian Harry Mallgrave writes, "more so than in other arts, prompts not only the simulation of its materials and forms, but also the anticipation of wanting to move within it. In a very basic way, a building, or a city for that matter, invites movement."[11]

I gave little thought to how any of this might pertain to spatial performance in sports until I took up fencing and refereeing soccer matches during the years when I taught architectural history at Carnegie Mellon University in Pittsburgh. In fencing, the dramatic flurries of lunge and riposte are set up by subtler sequences of threats and feints by which each fencer seeks to establish the optimal distance from which to strike, provoke the opponent to inadvertently create an unprotected opening, and maintain a safe distance from a counterattack. Like a well-designed building or the choreography of a dance performance, a fencing match concentrates awareness of the body's position in a spatial field, but in this instance, the physical setting measures only 14 meters long by 2 meters wide. The margin of success between scoring a touch and being scored upon is minuscule. On a larger scale, the relatively relaxed pace of the youth soccer matches that I officiated provided ample opportunity to reflect on the spatial patterns unfolding on the pitch. The youngest children would pursue the ball in a dense pack using only a fragment of the available field. As their skills improved and they learned to pass the ball, they became more aware of the pitch and how to take fuller advantage of the opportunities it afforded. They learned to "create space" with crossing passes to open new points of attack and to play the ball to gaps between opponents just in time for the arrival of an onrushing teammate. I realized that I could describe these tactics in terms of the fundamental spatial structures of compression and release familiar to me in both the ephemeral compositions of dancers and the more permanent constructions of architecture. At Carnegie Mellon and, subsequently, the University of Texas at Austin, I had the good fortune to work with students who played sports at high levels. They included golfers; baseball, basketball, volleyball, softball, football, and soccer players; climbers; sailors; swimmers; and track-and-field athletes. Among their classmates were equally accomplished dancers and artists. This mix of creative complexity-makers generated lively discussions comparing the understanding of space they had honed as athletes and artists to the spatial concepts they were learning in their architectural studies. They were in good company.

## ARTISTS AND ATHLETES

The Uruguayan writer Eduardo Galeano links spatial invention in soccer and sculpture in his account of the Basque artist Eduardo Chillida. As a young man, Chillida was a goalkeeper for Real Sociedad, the La Liga soccer club based in his hometown, San Sebastián, until a severe knee injury ended his career in 1943. "Chillida," Galeano writes, "bid goodbye to soccer and saw no alternative but to become a sculptor" (he studied architecture along the way). Characterizing the artist's striking compositions in concrete, stone, and steel, he observes, "Chillida works with materials so heavy they sink into the earth, but his powerful hands toss iron and reinforced concrete into the air where they discover other spaces and create new dimensions on the fly. He used to do the same thing with his body."[12]

A goalkeeper must protect an opening measuring 24 feet across by 8 feet high. Unable to cover this expanse from a fixed position, keepers anticipate the angle and timing of an attack and move quickly to be in just the right place to block a shot. In so doing, they hold their bodies, sometimes with arms outstretched, to appear large and distract the shooter's eye from the empty net. When the shot comes, they may need to fling themselves across the goal with arms and legs fully extended to make a fingertip deflection. Viewed as a freeze frame, the keeper's body presents a striking composition of mass, balance,

Figure 0.1. Eduardo Chillida, *Elogio del Horizonte*, 1990, Gijón, Spain. Roberto Sueiras Revuetta/Wikimedia Commons.

and space. Chillida explored these relationships in sculptures such as his *Elogio del Horizonte* (1990), which overlooks the Bay of Biscay from the Parque del Cerro de Santa Catalina in Gijón, Spain (figure 0.1). Made of reinforced concrete, the massive piece, 10 meters high, consists of two blocky piers that support a nearly circular beam, open at the ends like welcoming arms toward approaching visitors. While this description accounts for the components of the piece, it doesn't capture the aesthetically compelling contrasts of solid and void and stability and indeterminacy that frame our relationship to the unbroken horizon of the ocean. The shape, timing, and risk of a goalkeeper's diving save also can elicit aesthetic responses from spectators, but in the context of a soccer game, the aesthetic follows from the keeper's essential objective in the service of the game. Works of art are explicitly aesthetic.

In 1915, the Russian artist Kazimir Malevich produced a series of paintings demonstrating an approach to nonrepresentational art that he termed Suprematism. On display at the Art Institute of Chicago is one of these works, titled *Painterly Realism of a Football Player—Color Masses in the 4th Dimension* (figure 0.2). It presents a composition on a white background

Figure 0.2. Kazimir Malevich, *Painterly Realism of a Football Player—Color Masses in the 4th Dimension*, 1915, the Art Institute of Chicago. Steeve-x-art/Alamy.

of colored geometric shapes consisting of a square and three rectangles, a trapezoid, and two lines that converge on a small, green circle. The "painterly realism" is not in the depiction of a soccer player as such but in the relationships of form, color, and space that Malevich distilled from the dynamic flow of soccer matches. The title's reference to the fourth dimension, a fascination of many modernists at the time, underscores his belief that representations of these relationships could inspire viewers to see beyond familiar modes of perception.[13]

Another modernist who employed the spatial framework of a sport in a statement of transcendental order was the French-Swiss architect Le Corbusier. In his book *The City of To-morrow and Its Planning*, published in 1929, he writes, "When man is free, his tendency is towards pure geometry. It is then that he achieves what we call order." Expanding on the point, he asserts, "Human order, a geometrical thing . . . is the mark of great

Figure 0.3. Tennis players. Le Corbusier, *The City of To-morrow and Its Planning* (New York, 1929), 24.

civilizations."[14] While the wording of this passage in a book on urban design might prompt thoughts of the monumental boulevards and public squares of Paris, the symmetrical allées of the gardens of Versailles, or Le Corbusier's own visionary schemes for cities, he chose to illustrate the text with a photograph of a tennis match (figure 0.3).[15] Printed in high contrast, the black-and-white image emphasizes the nested rectangles delineated by the court markings, which resemble the guide lines (he referred to them as *tracés régulateurs*) that demarcate proportional relationships in Le Corbusier's architectural drawings. The scene is animated by two players dressed in tennis whites: one extends his body to play a shot; the other, standing on the baseline, has shifted his stance in anticipation of the return. They are Le Corbusier's avatars of free, enlightened persons who embrace the geometry of modernity in body and mind.

Brought to life, and swapping tennis rackets for skis, these characters would be right at home on the rooftop slopes of CopenHill (also known as Amager Bakke), a towering waste treatment and energy production plant in Copenhagen, which opened in 2019 (figure 0.4). The stepped roofs, derived from the requirements of the industrial functions within, provide a scaffold for a variety of outdoor sports. There is a ski slope, a climbing wall, and tree-lined pathways for walkers and runners. A café offers après-ski refreshments. Described as a

Figure 0.4. CopenHill, Copenhagen. Bjarke Ingels Group (BIG), architect, opened 2019. Jochen Tack/Alamy.

model for "hedonistic sustainability" by the architect Bjarke Ingels, the structure entwines the spatial properties of playing fields and public infrastructure—entities typically regarded as incompatible.[16]

Athletes at all levels test the mastery of their bodies in space. So do dancers, and it is no surprise to find correspondences between sports and dance.[17] This can be literal in the cases of sports with choreographed performances, such as figure skating, synchronized swimming, and gymnastics, and of dance choreography incorporating sports moves. For the dance number "Shoeless Joe from Hannibal, Mo." in the 1955 Broadway musical *Damn Yankees*, which hinges on the fortunes of a baseball team, Bob Fosse devised steps mimicking pitchers, batters, and fielders scooping up ground balls that invite comparisons of the athleticism of dancers and the grace of athletes. Twyla Tharp addressed this topic directly in a two-minute dance she made in 1980 for the ABC television series *Omnibus*.[18] "Dance Is a Man's Sport, Too" features Tharp, the New York City Ballet principal dancer Peter Martins, and the Pittsburgh Steelers' wide receiver Lynn Swann performing together on a studio set designed by Santo Loquasto that evokes a football gridiron.

Besides the promotional value of their celebrity, Swann and Martins were well-paired representatives of their respective worlds of sports and ballet. The feints, extensions, and leaping catches that Swann had perfected as a wide receiver parallel the elegant footwork, elongated lines, and aerials for which Martins was known. In addition, Swann had many years of training in a variety of dance forms, including ballet. As choreographer, Tharp applied her artistry for expressing the aesthetic potential of ordinary movements through the vocabulary of athletic and balletic steps that she created for the piece. The white-clad performers moving across the geometric lines of the setting echo the image of the tennis players in Le Corbusier's *City of To-morrow* but without attendant claims of transcendent order. Tharp's focus is direct appreciation of the ways the performers use their bodies. At one point, Martin executes a twisting jump (*tour jeté*) and Swann follows by miming a leaping catch. The sequence is shown in slow motion and freeze-frame against a backdrop marked with lines to highlight the "big air" of the jumps and, more subtly, the differences of form conditioned by the men's respective training (Swann, incidentally, caught more air than Martin).

## ARCHITECTURE OF THE PLAYING FIELD

In their respective ways, sports, the visual arts, architecture, and dance appeal to our predilection for complexity by manipulating our perception of physical space and inspiring a heightened sense of aesthetic awareness. Without imposing a restrictive category, such as designating sports as art, a contentious topic for philosophers of sport, I suggest that related inquiries in one domain can inspire new readings in others while respecting the unique qualities of each.[19] The *Sports Center* fan, the architecture enthusiast, and the balletomane have more to discuss than they may think.

This book contributes to such conversations by examining spatial practices in sports with respect to settings, mediated experience, performance, and social contexts.[20] In chapter 1,

I treat the settings for sports as architecture that frames constraints and opportunities for action. Like buildings, playing fields and courts project potential when empty and come to life when inhabited. The settings for global sports such as soccer and basketball are so familiar as to appear timeless, but their iconic configurations are more often the accumulated results of trial and error rather than singular masterstrokes, reflecting tradeoffs of custom and changing modes of play.

Like many people, much of my experience as a spectator is mediated by print, radio, televisual, and digital technologies that allow me to witness games remotely—live or after the fact. These technologies do more than transcribe a sporting event. Their representations of the proceedings impose a virtual architecture that reframes the setting of a sport and shapes the way spectators and players alike perceive the competition. Chapter 2 examines how mediating technologies color emotional response, introduce new points of view, and reorder time. Televisual media have increasingly augmented our perception of the action on the field with layers of information ranging from statistical data, such as measures of performance and probabilities of outcomes, to graphics highlighting the slope of a green on a golf course or the distance required for a first down on a football field. Formerly limited to spectatorship, technologies of mediation now shape the experience of athletes and officials on the field. Athletes can observe aspects of the game projected on giant video screens above their heads while officials utilize replays and automated monitoring systems to review close calls.

The referee's whistle and the baseball umpire's shout "Play ball!" activate temporary social spaces that, for the duration of the game, operate apart from the ordinary rhythms of daily life. Chapter 3 addresses the performance of athletes and spectators within this extraordinary realm. On the field, players and coaches exercise athletic prowess and tactical imagination to exploit the opportunities afforded by the game's rules and setting. The field of play becomes a laboratory of spatial invention where ideas promising competitive advantage are tested and revised. Alongside practices that can be described in material terms—play diagrams, achievements summarized as statistics—are the subjective experiences of perception and engagement. The dimensions of a soccer pitch do not change during a game, but players occupy it in ways that make it appear larger or smaller to their teammates and opponents. The flow of play can draw players and spectators alike into a state of aesthetic engagement—of being in the moment. Aesthetic engagement, a concept used by the disciplines of phenomenology, everyday aesthetics, and philosophy of sport, provides a conceptual platform that allows us to consider quantitative achievement and qualitative experience outside of oppositional binaries such as utility versus beauty or high culture versus low. It facilitates viewing sports alongside other highly focused experiences ranging from encounters with works of art or the natural world to affecting moments in daily life.

However much the social space of a sporting event may operate apart from the rhythm and conduct of ordinary life, it remains tethered to broader sociocultural constructions. Commercial interests govern professional and collegiate sports; nationalist and political interests color international and domestic competitions; conventions of gender, race, and class can restrict access for athletes and spectators. Familiar manifestations of such interests include patriotic displays, commercial logos adorning athletic apparel and equipment, and the demographics of teams and spectators. Chapter 4 examines how they are expressed spatially. The settings and performances of sports transform locations into places resonant with personal and collective meaning that can linger long after the game's final whistle. These practices can be uplifting and transformative, engaging players and spectators alike in the rejuvenation of communities, but they also can be used by social gatekeepers to exclude persons who do not conform to rigid notions of a "right way" of play. Some sports, however, foster a culture of disrupting normative practices. Appropriating urban landscapes as their fields of play, practitioners of parkour and skateboarding displace conventions of use, representation, and behavior in their exploration of the material properties and purpose of park benches and stair railings. The epilogue recapitulates the chapters' themes with respect to the trajectory of another, initially disruptive sport: snowboard halfpipe riding.

"This is a simple game," Skip, the manager of the minor-league Durham Bulls admonishes his hapless team in the classic baseball movie *Bull Durham* (1988): "You throw the ball, you hit the ball, you catch the ball." The objectives of other sports can be condensed in similarly reductive terms, but unnecessary obstacles complicate these simple-sounding tasks in compelling ways. Rural baseball diamonds and their counterparts—backyard hockey rinks, playground soccer pitches, streetball courts—may not bedazzle the eye like a storied professional or college stadium, but all are sites of multivalent spatial practices that begin with a physical frame, whether scratched in the dirt or elaborately defined, that is brought to life as an embodied social space of invention and memory.

CHAPTER I

# FRAMES

In October 2019 the Professional Squash Association held its Women's World Championship in a dazzling venue erected for the occasion in Giza, Egypt (figure 1.1). The portable, glass-enclosed court stood against the majestic backdrop of the ancient pyramids. At night, it was illuminated in such a way that the walls dematerialized. Spectators viewed the athletes competing in an ethereal, ordered space juxtaposed dramatically with the massive, Platonic solids commanding the background. At very different scales, the pyramids and squash court frame and structure the performance of human activities. The pyramids, built for the ages, anchored the rituals of a royal necropolis. The squash court, assembled and dismantled in a matter of days, celebrated the feats of the living according to the ritualistic practices of the sport.

Playing fields orient players, coaches, and officials with respect to location, opportunity, and limits. Their remarkable variety of configurations include the circle-in-the-square of the sumo *dohyō*, the emphatic order of the American football gridiron, the picturesque pathways of golf courses, and the abrupt dimensional reorientation of pole-vaulting pits. Whether defined by walls, painted lines, or the widely spaced buoys of a sailing race, playing fields manifest the unnecessary obstacles that the philosopher of sports Bernard Suits posits as fundamental to the constitution of sports.[1] They also contribute to a sport being "something in itself," in Karl Ove Knausgaard's words regarding frames, by demarcating an inside and an outside.[2] Within the boundaries of the frame, special rules of behavior apply that contribute to the formation of a discrete social space.

Figure 1.1. Nour El Sherbini vs. Raneem El Welily, PSA Women's Squash World Championship, Giza, Egypt, November 1, 2019. Omar Zoheiry/dpa/Alamy.

The ubiquity of the playing fields of popular sports such as baseball, soccer, and basketball can lead us to take their features for granted. While the stadiums and arenas that house them may be hailed as "wonders of the world" (at least by publicists) and involve celebrated architects and engineers, playing fields are designed and constructed largely out of the public eye.[3] With the notable exception of links designed by golf course architects employing signature styles, playing fields are products of largely anonymous processes characteristic of vernacular buildings and landscapes (the ordinary built environment). Their configurations reflect institutional consensus and are valued for typological consistency. Rarely known beyond the circles of professional trade associations, their makers are members of a building culture involving networks of sports officials, craftspersons, material suppliers, and manufacturers. On occasion, technical innovation may bring attention to their work, as in the case of the recently introduced LED glass surfaces that turn basketball courts into dazzling video displays and the retractable natural grass football fields that roll outdoors at the domed State Farm Stadium (2006) in Glendale, Arizona, and Allegiant Stadium (2020) in Las Vegas, Nevada. Performance failures, such as the slippery field conditions at the 2023 Super Bowl held in Glendale, bring undesired attention.[4]

While the ability to build and maintain playing fields at elite venues requires great expertise and large budgets, general knowledge of their configuration is widespread and broadly applicable. A person with even casual experience can relationally set out the essential features of a rudimentary hockey rink, soccer pitch, or baseball diamond. We often acquire such engrained knowledge in childhood, passed down orally and through emulation of older children and adults. Dissemination may be limited to a narrow cultural or geographic range—hurling in Ireland, for instance—or be global, as in the case of soccer pitches and basketball courts.

The baseball field in Ashton, Wisconsin, a tiny rural crossroads community near Madison, illustrates the application of such embedded knowledge in a setting far removed from the bright lights of American Family Field in Milwaukee, home of Major League Baseball's (MLB) Brewers (figure 1.2). The community consists of the church, school, and cemetery of St. Peter's Catholic Parish, a scattering of houses, and Connie's Home Plate tavern (a ubiquitous feature of Wisconsin towns of any size). St. Peter's Park is across the road from the parish buildings. It includes a snack shack proudly proclaiming the "Home of Ashton Baseball," an equipment shed, wooden benches for the teams, a backstop, and a few low bleachers and picnic tables for spectators. A cornfield lies just beyond the outfield fence. The bucolic scene recalls the movie *Field of Dreams*, but apart from this cinematic association, the ordinariness of the field doesn't compel the attention of passersby. Far more remarkable from the conventional perspective of monumentality in architecture and landscape architecture are the Gothic Revival church (1901) and the cemetery across the street.

Approached from a broader and more synthetic perspective of spatial practices, however, St. Peter's Park offers much to talk about. It is both a very local place and part of the broader fabric of baseball. Like the traditional, basilican plan of the parish church across the street, the layout of the ballfield represents an enduring spatial type with a history spanning almost two

Figure 1.2. St. Peter's Park, Ashton, Wisconsin. Photograph by author.

hundred years (far less, certainly, than the two millennia of Christian basilicas, but rich, nonetheless). The typological features, including the overall shape and principal components, such as bases and pitching mound, link Ashton to other ballparks from sandlots to major league stadiums. Embedded within the ubiquity of type are particulars that reflect local histories and uses. The dimensions of Ashton's infield and the distance to the outfield fence (328 feet in center field) indicate that it was built primarily as a venue for adult baseball rather than softball or youth baseball. The shape of the outfield along the fence follows the property line of the neighboring cornfield.

Operating on a shoestring budget in Wisconsin's amateur Home Talent Baseball League, the Ashton A's draw on the diverse skills of team members and friends to maintain the field, benches, and sheds. The current manager, Dave Adler, leads upkeep and improvements based on his fifty years of experience with the team, which he joined as a teenager.[5] When grading is required to improve drainage or eliminate irregularities, he turns to people in the community for Bobcats and other machinery, materials, and labor. He and the players hold in

Figure 1.3. Rossella Fiamingo (*left*) vs. Maya Lawrence, Women's Épée Individual competition, London 2012 Summer Olympics. PA Images/Alamy.

their minds the ideal properties of ballparks and realize them as best they can with the resources at their disposal. Unoccupied for much of the week, St. Peter's Park comes to life on Sunday afternoons in the late spring and summer. The umpire's call "Play ball!" activates the field as a social space governed by the game's rules of time and behavior. Counterparts to Ashton's ballpark can be found among venues of amateur sports around the world.[6]

Playing fields frame boundaries and spatial orientation. In the 110-meter track race or the 50-meter sprint in swimming, the frame is a narrow lane that separates opponents and defines a linear trajectory from starting block to finish line. Modern fencing is played on a narrow strip, the piste, 14 meters long by 1.5 to 2 meters wide (figure 1.3). This narrow, linear frame corresponds to the profile stance fencers assume to minimize exposure to the opponent's blade. Fencing bouts do not have a directional objective other than establishing the critical distance for scoring a touch, but a fencer may attempt to force the opponent into an awkward position at the end of the strip. The rectangular shape of a soccer pitch also orients the game longitudinally, in this case toward the goal at each end, but its size and broad proportions allow the freedom of movement—lengthwise, side to side, and diagonally—that is a fundamental characteristic of the sport. Gates set in the swirling whitewater of a canoe slalom course must be navigated in sequence according to prescribed directions—downstream for green gates, upstream for red gates. Their placement complements the hydraulic forces of the stream in determining the competition's level of complexity. The uneven parallel bars in artistic gymnastics frame movement in three dimensions as the gymnast maneuvers from bar to bar, back and forth, up and down, executing a prescribed set of flight maneuvers, grip changes, and turns. Each sport imposes spatial constraints that challenge athletes' tactical inventiveness and physical prowess.

"The world of sports with its geometries and synthetic surfaces," the cultural geographer John Bale writes, "simplifies the world of nature."[7] He points out how the logics of fair play and comparative performance require consistent conditions from venue to venue. Portable, factory-built, glass-walled squash courts and synthetic turf exemplify this ideal. Golf courses, while often designed with attention to differentiation and the appearance of naturalness, simplify the world of nature through the management of topography and plantings to facilitate certain qualities of play. Bale correlates the standardization of playing fields with the institutionalization of sports and broader sociological dimensions that go beyond the immediate requirements of athletic competition.[8] For example, as we shall see in chapter 4, William George Beers, instrumental in the appropriation and transformation of the Indigenous peoples' game of lacrosse into the national sport of Anglo Canada, viewed field boundaries in moralizing terms as the expression of "that mark of civilization and trespass, the fence."[9] More prosaic motivations pertain to maintaining public order and monetization.

For a closer look at the variety and production of the frames created for sports, we'll examine the playing fields of baseball, soccer, and American football; the courts of squash and basketball; and the courses of golf. Spatially, a baseball field comprises a set of nested frames that shape the game in distinct ways. Football gridirons and soccer pitches represent divergent approaches to structuring the flow of play on similarly sized rectangular fields. Modern squash courts illustrate the long histories of trial and error and adaptation that underlie the dimensions of the playing fields of many sports. The spatial divisions of basketball courts reflect changing styles of play. Golf courses pose puzzles for players to solve to the best of their abilities.

## THE NESTED FRAMES OF BASEBALL

Americans commonly speak of baseball being played on a diamond in a ballpark (figure 1.4). The latter term, to which I will return in chapter 4, evokes the sport's bucolic mythology. The former describes the principal feature of the playing field: a square rotated to present a diamond with respect to the batter's position at the corner designated as home plate. This layout wasn't inevitable. An early version of baseball in the mid-nineteenth century known as the Massachusetts Game or Town Ball oriented the square orthogonally so that the batter stood midway on a line between first base and fourth base (home).[10] The diamond was a feature of the rival, and ultimately

Figure 1.4. PNC Park, Pittsburgh. Populous, architect, opened 2001. Chris LaBasco/Alamy.

dominant, New York Game. The two arrangements framed the game differently. The square of the Massachusetts Game was more omnidirectional in keeping with that game's wide-open play, in which the ball could be hit fair in any direction, much like cricket. The diamond, on the other hand, simultaneously frames the action toward the outfield within the angle of first and third baselines, toward the infield by the complementary angle formed by the corner of the square at second base, and toward the rotational movement of baserunners.

The infield diamond is the most pronounced of a series of nested frames composing an MLB field. It is a place of measure. The bases are set 90 feet apart; the rubber slab on the pitcher's mound (itself rigidly specified as to height and shape) is 60 feet, 6 inches from home plate.[11] The locations of the bases and the pitching rubber, which demarcates the pitcher's position on the mound, have been codified since the end of the nineteenth century, the result of trial and error to balance opportunities for the offense and defense. Remarkably, even though many players today can run faster and throw harder than their predecessors, the balance has not been upset. A batter hitting an infield chopper has a chance of safely reaching first base if a quirky bounce forces an infielder to take an extra step or juggle the transfer of the ball from glove to throwing hand. A baserunner on first base can still steal second by carefully assessing the pitcher's timing and pitch selection. Superimposed on the infield diamond are markings that regulate play, including the batter's boxes flanking home plate, the coaching boxes at first and third bases, and the running lane along the first base line.

The rules of baseball standardize the dimensions of the diamond in the spirit of consistency and fair play, but in practice, the pursuit of competitive advantage can test the boundaries of these ideals. There is much lore regarding groundskeepers making surreptitious alterations intended to improve the chances of the home team.[12] In *Men at Work: The Craft of Baseball,* George Will writes of the unusually ambitious effort of the San Francisco Giants in a series played at home against the rival Los Angeles Dodgers in August 1962. To counter the threat of the Dodgers' lightning-quick Maury Wills stealing second base, the Giants' groundskeeper, Matty Schwab, replaced the soil in the area where Wills was expected to lead off first base with a spongy mix of well-watered peat and sand. The "speed trap" didn't alter the frame's statutory 90 feet between the bases but worked as planned by increasing the risk of an attempted steal (a tactic the Giants were willing to forego to thwart their opponents).[13]

In contrast to the standardized features of the infield, the configuration of the outfield is subject to few regulations. The rules of MLB do not specify its shape beyond defining its edges as extensions of the first and third baselines and prescribing minimum dimensions for enclosing fences. For stadiums built after 1958 (the year the Brooklyn Dodgers moved into Los Angeles Memorial Coliseum, which had a very shallow left field), these are 325 feet along the first base and third base lines and 400 feet from home plate to center field. This flexibility allows for the design of asymmetrical outfields, often determined by property boundaries. In the early twentieth century, team owners shoehorned urban ballparks into irregularly shaped lots, resulting in quirky layouts with angle changes along outfield fence lines that could cause unexpected ricochets or deaden balls in a corner.[14] Fenway Park in Boston, wedged alongside Lansdowne Street in 1912, features an unusually shallow left field (310 feet) with a towering wall, famously known as the Green Monster. In such circumstances, teams play the park as well their opponents.

In the second half of the twentieth century, most of these ballparks were replaced by larger stadiums built on less constrained sites created by urban redevelopment projects or in suburban locations. Symmetry rather than idiosyncrasy characterized the layout of outfields. Impressive as they appeared in architects' renderings and aerial photography, parks such as Shea Stadium in New York (1964), Busch Memorial Stadium in St. Louis (1966), Three Rivers Stadium in Pittsburgh (1970), and Riverfront Stadium in Cincinnati (1970), which accommodated football as well as baseball, had a blandness and a lack of intimacy that dismayed many commentators and fans. "Too distant," Roger Angell wrote of Shea Stadium in the *New Yorker*, ". . . this imposed geometry keeps the elevated fan forever distant from the doings within the contained square of the outfield."[15] Oriole Park at Camden Yards in Baltimore (1992) inspired a new generation of more intimate, single-purpose "retro-ballparks" that deliberately incorporated asymmetrical outfields as character-defining features.

Alongside irregular geometries, outfielders have had to negotiate the presence of obstacles within their workplaces. The outfield at Old Yankee Stadium included, in addition to the dimensional quirks due to its urban site in the Bronx, monuments to deceased players and managers in deep center field that were in bounds until 1975. Minute Maid Park, the home of the Houston Astros, had until 2017 a flagpole and a steep, 30-degree incline known as Tal's Hill just inside the center field fence. In the college game, an even greater anomaly was Billy Goat Hill in Clark Field (1928–1974) at the University of Texas at Austin. It was a rocky outcropping in fair territory in deep right field where the Longhorns' practiced agility climbing "goat paths" to retrieve long drives constituted a unique form of home-field advantage.

The smallest but most important of baseball's nested frames is defined by home plate. A baseball game begins with a batter stepping up to the plate to await the pitcher's throw and does not end until one team scores more runs than the other after an equal number of chances. In the sport's formative days, home was an iron disk painted white. In 1868, the circle was replaced by a square slab of stone or white marble rotated in alignment with the infield diamond.[16] The familiar five-sided plate became regulation in the 1900 season. Made of hard, white-colored rubber (less slick when wet than a marble slab), its shape nestles within the vertex of the first and third baselines and presents the pitcher with a side 17 inches wide.[17] The arrangement makes it easier to follow the trajectory of the ball across the strike zone, a spatial construction that is geometric, dimensionally variable, and intangible.

Every time a batter prepares to face a pitch, players, umpires, and spectators alike must visualize the strike zone as a pentagonal volume floating above the plate (figure 1.5). While the fixed

Figure 1.5. Baseball strike zone. Diagram by author. Arthur Didyk/Shutterstock.

dimensions of home plate establish the width of the zone, the batter's body determines its height. The strike zone is contested territory, which the pitcher and batter duel to control. A pitch passing through the zone is a strike, counted against the batter; a pitch outside it is a ball, counted against the pitcher. Neatly summarizing the pitcher's objective, the manager Casey Stengel said of the ace Satchel Paige, who played both in the Negro Leagues and in MLB, "He threw the ball as far from the bat and as close to the plate as possible."[18] Bob Gibson, a former pitcher for the St. Louis Cardinals, offered a more exacting description. "The middle 12 [inches] belong to the hitter. The inside and outside ½ are mine. If I pitch to spots properly, there's no way the batter is going to hit the ball hard consistently."[19] Fiercely determined to maintain that territorial division, Gibson responded to batters who had the audacity to reach across the strike zone by throwing the next pitch high and inside. Egregious offenders would suffer more painful consequences.

In 1876, batters were allowed to call for a pitch that would be "high," crossing the plate at a height between their shoulder and waist; "low," between their waist and at least one foot above the plate; or "fair," anywhere between their shoulder height and one foot above the ground.[20] A decade later, the segmented strike zone was replaced by a single zone extending from the shoulder to the knee, and the prerogative for selecting the placement of the pitch shifted from the batter to the pitcher. Over the years, numerous rule changes have reduced the height of the zone (a revision in 1969 was partially inspired by Gibson's domination of batters). Currently, MLB defines the zone as "that area over home plate the upper limit of which is a horizontal line at the midpoint between the top of the shoulders and the top of the uniform pants, and the lower level is a line at the hollow beneath the kneecap," which must be determined by "the batter's stance as the batter is prepared to swing at a pitched ball."[21]

In the present age of numerically quantified specification, the strike zone is an anachronistic mix of precision and approximation. Umpires must adjust for the height and stance of each batter while maintaining consistency in their application of the rule. Players, coaches, and fans are known to take exception to the accuracy of these assessments (and to the acuity of the plate umpire's eyesight). Automated systems for calling balls and strikes by tracking the path of the ball with respect to biometric data stored for each player promise greater precision, but despite providing consistency within the algorithmic parameters, their results will continue to have a degree of approximation subject to a margin of error, even if slight.[22] They also introduce an external agent to the determination of a spatial frame that throughout the game's history has been defined by human actors on the field.

Measuring 17 inches wide (the width of home plate) and approximately 20 inches high (depending on the batter's physique), the strike zone is the focal point of players, officials, and spectators. In the duel between pitcher and batter, the pitcher attempts to deceive the batter's perception of the ball's trajectory by employing an arsenal of pitches with names evocative of their aerodynamic properties and techniques—slider, curveball, fastball, cutter, and knuckleball. The batter, facing a 3-inch ball thrown just 60 feet away at speeds that can exceed 100 miles per hour, must anticipate the pitcher's predilections and differentiate pitches that can be hit cleanly, ignored as balls outside the zone, or cleared out of the zone by any means possible to keep their turn at bat alive.

When the bat makes contact with the pitched ball, the focus of the game expands from the concentrated space of the strike zone to the larger frames of the infield, outfield, and even beyond the limits of the ballpark in the case of a home run hit over the fences. The batter becomes a base runner who must make the counterclockwise trip around the diamond, avoiding perils such as a sure-handed shortstop turning a double play or being caught in a rundown between opponents blocking his path to the safety of a base.[23] For their part, defenders must regain control of the ball and thwart the base runners' advances. Outfielders, playing the ball 300 feet or more from home plate, collapse the space opened by the batter with long, precise throws to the smaller frame of the infield, where their teammates retire the base runner or cede possession of a base. The nested frames of strike zone, infield, and outfield constitute an architecture that shapes the game at three different scales, each of which has its own unit of reference: the relationship of home plate and the batter's body, the distance between bases, and the boundary condition of the outfield wall.

## CONTESTED TERRITORY: SOCCER PITCHES AND FOOTBALL GRIDIRONS

Soccer and American football belong to a family of team invasion ball sports that includes rugby, Australian football, and Canadian football. Their object is the conquest of an opponent's territory by delivering the ball into a guarded area located at the end of the longitudinally oriented field, which is rectangular except for the oval of Australian football, a legacy of the game having been played on cricket grounds in its formative years. As these closely related sports were codified in the second half of the nineteenth century, their respective fields acquired distinct features that regulate play and pose spatial challenges. The soccer pitch and the American football gridiron illustrate the development of these frames.

Standardization of the soccer pitch was led by the Football Association (FA) in Great Britain. Promptly after its founding in 1863, the organization published rules that underlie the *Laws of the Game,* which govern the sport today. The FA's initial specifications for the pitch simply limited its dimensions to a maximum length of 200 yards and a maximum breadth of 100 yards (approximately twice the size of the modern field), marked at the corners by flags. The goals consisted of freestanding upright posts, 8 yards apart, a distance that has not changed. The crossbar and netting are later additions.[24] Given the long distance between the corner flags, early players approximated the boundaries of the pitch until the introduction of ground markings in 1882 that demarcated the touch (sideline) and goal lines (end lines). Subsequently, additional markings articulated certain regulations (figure 1.6). The center circle, halfway line, and goal and penalty areas were introduced by the early twentieth century, and the penalty arcs were added in 1937. The *Laws of the Game* specify the locations of these features but allow the overall dimensions of the pitch to vary within minimum and maximum ranges (90–120 meters in length, 45–90 meters in width), providing the length exceeds the width.

Figure 1.6. Soccer pitch, Mühlheim an der Ruhr, Germany. Hans Blossey/Alamy.

Beyond designating "in play" from "out of play" and separating players and spectators, the touch and goal lines have tactical implications. By dribbling along a touch line, a player can use the boundary to limit the angles of attack available to opponents seeking to gain possession of the ball. The interior angles of the corners of the pitch can be used to similar advantage. A familiar tactic in the waning moments of a match is for a team with a narrow lead to kill time (and the hopes of opposing players and fans) by closely guarding the ball in the confined space of a corner of the opponent's territory.[25] The internal field markings facilitate the management of the game with respect to player positioning, the special rules pertaining to the goal areas, and the administration of penalties, but do not otherwise dictate the flow of the game to the degree imposed by the markings of American football fields.

The defining features of American football as a battle over the measured conquest of territory distinct from soccer and rugby were codified in the 1880s and 1890s by the Intercollegiate Football Association, composed of Ivy League schools. Key elements to the development of the game were the concept of the line of scrimmage from which each play begins, introduced in 1880, and acceptance two years later of the downs-and-distance rule proposed by the Yale University player Walter Camp (later a coach for Yale and Stanford).[26] It stipulates the number of attempts (downs) for a team to advance the ball a minimum distance to retain possession (initially, three downs to make 5 yards; extended to four downs and 10 yards by 1906). These innovations established the shifting frame—the distance required to maintain possession—within the larger frame of the field that underlies the game's character as a contest of strength and wits to displace the opposing players.

An early objection in the debates regarding Camp's down-and-distance proposal warned of the difficulty the referee would face in measuring distances accurately. He reportedly responded, "The field can be marked with lines five yards apart." Amid the dismissive laughter, someone quipped, "It would look like a gridiron."[27] Little did they know. By the early twentieth century, the length and width of the 100-yard by 160-foot field

Figure 1.7. Syracuse University stadium, Syracuse, New York. Postcard, 1910.

were subdivided by a grid of lines drawn at 5-yard intervals, inspiring the term *gridiron* (figure 1.7). The lines parallel to the goal line (in use by 1882) calibrated a team's progress toward the goal. Those parallel to the sidelines (in use by 1906) provided references for governing the positions of players in plays involving the newly legalized forward pass. They were replaced by the 1930s with the pair of dashed lines—hash marks—that guide the placement of the ball for each play (a ball downed between the hash mark and the sideline is placed on the hash mark).

Upon this rigidly structured landscape, on-field officials quantify the violent, tumultuous struggle for territorial advantage with measurements of down and distance. A fraction of an inch can be the difference between the team on offense gaining a new set of downs or forfeiting the ball to the opponents. Assessments of these gains or losses are performed by a crew of sideline assistants who, like old-fashioned land surveyors, manipulate a 10-yard measuring chain (now assisted by video replay review). In contrast, soccer referees assess the 10-yard distance fixing the position of defenders at the start of a free kick by eye. Rather than dimensional precision, the critical issues are to assure an unimpeded kick and to maintain the flow of the game.

Spatially, the playing fields of soccer, football, and related sports offer players an open expanse for movement constrained by the peripheral presence of the boundary and regulatory lines at their feet, which might be thought of as virtual walls. The playing field for squash, on the other hand, situates its players within a tightly confined area bound by physical walls.

## FITTING IN: THE EVOLUTION OF THE SQUASH COURT

Squash is played in a room (figure 1.8), which may be part of a building or a temporary, freestanding structure such as the glass court erected at Giza that I described earlier. The *Specifications for Squash Courts*, published by the sport's governing body, the World Squash Federation (WSF), runs twenty-five pages and addresses construction details as well as dimensions (limiting tolerances to 10 millimeters along the walls, for instance) and locations of markings.[28] Walls must be able to withstand the impact of players' bodies, quantified by assumptions of mass, speed, and coefficients of absorption; construction joints must not be wider than 2 millimeters in the plane of the wall surface; no more than three different colors may be used on the wall playing surfaces, and all colors must have a minimum reflective value of 50 percent. In addition to publishing specifications, the WSF maintains a directory of accredited products ranging from flooring systems to wall surfaces to LED lighting. Exemplifying the sport's modern institutional structure, this dimensional precision codifies features evolved by a vernacular process of custom and feel.

As James Zug recounts in *Squash: A History of the Game*, the sport originated in the mid-nineteenth century at the Harrow School in Greater London.[29] It evolved from an informal game played in the school's irregularly shaped courtyards by younger students developing skills to compete in the upperclassmen's sport of rackets (not to be confused with the modern sport of racquetball), which was played throughout the British Empire on purpose-built, rectangular, walled courts. In 1865,

Figure 1.8. Squash court. Tito Wong/Shutterstock.

the school opened new courts for rackets (the historic indoor court remains in use) and fives (a version of handball played on a smaller court than rackets), and squash players appropriated the latter for indoor matches. The game quickly spread beyond the precincts of the Harrow School.

In the United States, the initial point of diffusion was St. Paul's School in Concord, New Hampshire.[30] Headmaster Jay Conover had encountered squash and rackets in Montréal and introduced the games to his school (along with ice hockey). In addition to a rackets court, he commissioned four open-air squash courts that were dedicated in 1884. Reportedly, they were modeled on the courts of the Harrow School using dimensions provided by a Harrow alumnus living in Cooperstown, New York. As other schools, athletic clubs, and private gyms adopted the game, squash courts were shoehorned into the attics and basements of buildings and made to fit alongside courts designed for rackets, squash tennis (played with a small tennis racket and a lawn tennis ball), and fives.

The improvisations led to considerable variation of court dimensions, but in the 1920s, the sport's governing bodies in the United Kingdom and the United States curtailed the range in their respective jurisdictions.[31] The Tennis, Racquets, and

Fives Association in the UK based its standard on the courts of the Bath Club in London, built in 1922. Measuring 32 feet long by 21 feet wide, these courts were well regarded by players using the soft ball favored in British squash. The United States Squash Racquets Association (USSRA) codified the slightly divergent evolution of the American game (Canadian squash courts have their own dimensional history), which was played with a harder, more lively ball on slightly smaller courts, 32 feet by 18½ feet, compatible with squash tennis and fives. The American and British modes of play were finally reconciled in the 1990s with acceptance of the 32-by-21-foot "international singles court" and use of the soft ball.

Alongside the regulation of court dimensions, the WSF's construction specifications evolved from a variety of localized practices. In the nineteenth and early twentieth centuries, stone, concrete, and wood were common materials for walls and floors depending on availability and the prevailing construction practices of local builders. Zug highlights two pivotal moments of inflection toward standardization in his account of the work of squash-playing American architect Paul Monaghan Jr.[32] Commissioned to design new courts for the Hill School in Pottstown, Pennsylvania, in 1954, Monaghan replaced the expensive and time-consuming American practice of facing the playing surface with approximately two thousand maple strips by adapting a system of prefabricated, interlocking maple panels (trade-named Doweloc) originally developed for truck-bed liners. Monaghan went on to serve the USSRA as consulting architect for improving court construction and performance using prefabricated, modular components. In 1968, he designed the first full-height, glass back wall for a court at the University of Pennsylvania. This was a key step toward the realization of the portable glass championship court, subsequently perfected by others, notably Playcon Recreational Equipment Ltd. of Kitchener, Ontario.[33] The crystalline courts erected at Giza and other championship venues are industrialized products of artisanal structures developed through trial and error.

Within the frame of floor and walls, squash courts have nested spaces. Lines on the floor and on the front wall regulate how the ball is put into play. Undefined in the rules is an area of great strategic significance for what comes next. This is the T position, or just T, which takes its name from the T shape formed at the intersection of the short line demarcating front court and back court and the half-court line that separates the service areas. From the centralized location of the T, a player commands a variety of options for directing the ball away from the opponent and quickly reaching other parts of the court to return a volley. Control of the T is a fundamental strategic objective and a hard-fought element of the game. Its importance is a consequence of the proportional relationship of the dimensions of the court with respect to the human body, a fit worked out by custom rather than predetermined rule.

## DOES THE KEY FIT? COMPETITIVE BALANCE ON THE BASKETBALL COURT

Basketball courts, like squash courts, are products of trial and revision, but more often than squash courts, changes to their configuration have been driven by strategic innovations, responses to overpowering levels of athletic performance, and what would make for a more appealing game.[34] When James Naismith invented the game in December 1891, its setting in the gymnasium of the YMCA International Training School in Springfield, Massachusetts, was a given, and his thirteen original rules focused on the mechanics of play rather than the playing field. Unstated was the position of the baskets, affixed pragmatically to the structure of the gym's running track 10 feet above the floor. Naismith subsequently explained his thinking behind what became the game's defining feature.[35] Seeking to emphasize skill over force in the confined space of the gymnasium, he elevated the baskets above the heads of the players to discourage goaltending and to require the ball to be shot in an arc rather than thrown in a straight line.

Early basketball rule books allowed much latitude in the configuration of courts (figure 1.9). Rule number 1 for the YMCA's North American Leagues published in *Spalding's*

Figure 1.9. University of Wisconsin–Madison freshman women's basketball team, Ladies Hall (now Chadbourne Hall) gymnasium. Photograph by Blanchard Harper, 1900. Wisconsin Historical Society, WHI-2263.

*Athletic Library* for the 1896–97 season simply states, "Basket Ball [*sic*] may be played on any grounds free from obstruction, said grounds not to exceed 3,500 square feet of actual playing space" (today's regulation NBA court is 4,700 square feet).[36] Boundaries were to be marked by a line, and there was to be a distance of at least 3 feet separating the side boundaries from enclosing walls or fences. Since baskets (specified as nets rather than the peach baskets Naismith originally used in Springfield) often were attached to walls, no separation was required at the ends of the court, which must have been scenes of painful crashes. Rule 3.1 set the height of the rim of the basket at 10 feet, as today; rule 11.2 specified demarcation of the center of the court (now the center circle); and rules 11.13–14 set out dimensions but did not require markings for the free throw lane that regulates the positioning of players for penalty shots. Standardization of court dimensions began in the 1920s (the modern NBA court measures 94 by 50 feet).

The first professional basketball game on record was played between teams sponsored by the Trenton and Brooklyn YMCAs in the third-floor social hall of the Masonic Temple in Trenton, New Jersey, on November 7, 1896. To provide separation in the crowded space between spectators and players and to avoid the melees that erupted when players fought to claim loose balls out of bounds, a 12-foot-high wire-mesh fence surrounded the court. Other professional teams playing in make-do settings adopted the practice, and the sight of "cagers" playing the ball (and each other) off the fence remained features of the professional game even after the revision of the out-of-bounds rule in 1902 and the use of venues with more spacious accommodations. Rope netting replaced wire, but the cage left its mark on players. Joel S. (Shikey) Gotthoffer, who played at the end of the cage era in the 1930s for the Nanticoke Nans in the Pennsylvania State League recalled, "I came home with the cage's markings on me. You could play ticktacktoe [*sic*] on everybody after a game because the cage marked you up."[37]

The modern regulation basketball court is marked by lines, circles, and arcs that have undergone much more continuous experimentation than the markings of squash courts, soccer pitches, and football fields (figure 1.10). Changes to the free throw lane and the introduction of the three-point arc have had particularly significant impact on the game.

The free throw lane was firmly established in the rule book by 1906. Originally 6 feet wide, the lane extends from the endline (baseline) to the free throw line, where the penalty shot is taken, 15 feet from the backboard. Hash marks along the sides of the lane indicate the positions the shooter's teammates and opponents may take. A circle extending the shooter's zone of protection surrounds the line. The likeness of the circle and the narrow lane to a keyhole inspired the name *key* for the zone.

The key today is 16 feet wide. Its history of expansion is tied not to the process of shooting free throws but to mitigating the play of certain dominating players in battles to control the area in front of the basket. The great center Wilt Chamberlain ruefully observed, "The world is made up of Davids. I am a Goliath. And nobody roots for Goliath."[38] Before Chamberlain's time, the Davids of the court had received a boost in 1936 from the implementation of a rule forbidding players on offense

Figure 1.10. Adidas Arena, Porte de La Chapelle, Paris. SCAU, architect, opened 2024. Abaca Press/Alamy.

from occupying the key for three seconds or more. The time constraint encouraged movement under the net but did not eliminate the dominance of a Goliath named George Mikan, whose space-filling play with the Minneapolis (now Los Angeles) Lakers in the late 1940s and early 1950s contributed to the instigation of the so-called Mikan Rule in 1951, which doubled the width of the lane from 6 to 12 feet. Chamberlain's similarly powerful play a decade later in Philadelphia and San Francisco with the Warriors (now the Golden State Warriors) inspired a second expansion to the present 16 feet.

The broad arc of the three-point line, nearly spanning the width of the court shortly beyond the free throw circle, demarcates the boundary between the area closer to the basket in which successful shots count two points and the outer expanse where they count three points. The three-point option was introduced as a regular feature of the game in the 1960s by the now defunct American Basketball, American Basketball Association (ABA), and Eastern Professional leagues. Their owners believed the incentive of the extra point would encourage players to attempt long-range shots, which they regarded as basketball's equivalent to the towering home runs in baseball, thereby adding excitement to the game and increasing its appeal to spectators. The National Basketball Association (NBA) eventually (and not to universal applause) added the three-point shot to its rulebook for the 1979–1980 season, and the National Collegiate Athletic Association followed suit in 1987. Arbitrarily adopting the ABA's division of the court, the NBA set the boundary as an arc in front of the basket with a radius of 23 feet, 9 inches and connected to lines 22 feet from the sides of the basket parallel to the lane (this leaves a 3-foot-wide area inside each sideline). Despite the owners' desire for a pyrotechnic display of game-winning long-range shots, the game did not change overnight, and, as I'll discuss in chapter 3, coaches and players struggled to incorporate the three-point line into their game strategies. For its part, the league experimented with the distance of the line from the basket, moving it 21 inches closer in 1994 and back to its original position three years later. The most suitable distance remains a topic of spirited conversation.[39]

The size of the court is another controversial matter. Some observers of the sport argue it is time to enlarge the court because today's players and playing styles have outgrown the confines of the frame established one hundred years ago.[40] They are willing to trade off the dimensional consistency of the playing field to make the game more aesthetically appealing by improving its flow.

## PUZZLES IN THE LANDSCAPE: THE ARCHITECTURE OF GOLF

Outdoor basketball courts, ballparks, and soccer pitches may be located in spectacular natural areas, but they typically are set apart from their surroundings by well-defined boundaries and playing surfaces dictated by the requirements of their respective sports. In architectural terms, they are self-referential objects in the landscape. The premises of some sports, however, engage athletes with challenging features of natural landscapes, or their representation. Alpine ski racing courses, for instance, are set with respect to the fall lines of mountain slopes (often subject to extensive manipulation). Surfing competitions are held at coastal sites presenting dynamic interactions of waves, winds, currents, and subsurface terrain. Urban parkour routes lead practitioners through features in cityscapes selected for qualities of shape, orientation, and texture that invite displays of graceful moves. Each in its way poses puzzles for players to solve. The design of golf courses can be particularly creative in this respect through the integration of topographical features, plantings, and prevailing winds.

The sandy linksland of Scotland's eastern coast, which drains well and historically did not have high agricultural value, offered suitable sites for early golf courses such as St. Andrews, where the game has been played for hundreds of years. Players determined the number and routing of holes in accordance with the offerings of natural features as targets. The notion of the course as an appropriation of the natural landscape continues to inspire design today, as does evocation of the sport's earliest courses in Scotland.[41] Such is the case of Erin Hills Golf Course (2006), the site of the 2017 US Open, which reinterprets the character of Scotland's traditional links courses in the disposition of fairways and greens laid out among the rolling drumlins, eskers, and kettles of eastern Wisconsin's Kettle Moraine region (figure 1.11). In the spirit of maintaining continuity from course to surroundings, the *Rules of Golf* allow boundary markings to be simple fences or posts that overlay the topography unobtrusively. Not all golf courses blend in. The emerald islands of courses built in desert landscapes are hubristic impositions on the native landscape.

Within the course boundaries, the familiar inventory of defined features, including tee boxes, hazards, and greens, was in place by the 1880s. Their specific forms and the overall dimensions of the course were then, as today, determined by each designer's subjective assessment of the degree of challenge and the aesthetic experience they offer players.

Golf course design initially was an informal affair of players and groundskeepers whose legacy survives in the wide fairways and routing of the Old Course at St. Andrews, but it began to be professionalized around the turn of the twentieth century. The

Figure 1.11. Erin Hills Golf Course, Erin, Wisconsin. Designed by Michael John Hurdzan, Dana Frey, and Ron Whitten, opened 2006. Photograph courtesy of Erin Hills.

designation of course designers as golf architects came into use by the 1920s. H. N. Wethered and T. Simpson made the case for the appellation in their treatise *The Architectural Side of Golf*, published in London in 1929. "Although golf architecture may be a curious and irregular form of architecture," they write, "it is architecture none the less. It has to do with building, planning and construction in as true a sense as the most ambitious works of genius with which the art is usually associated."[42] The authors go on to assert, "The task of the architect is therefore to create, if he can, this atmosphere of interest, to invent secrets that lie beneath the surface—even appearances that can be partly misleading. . . . And with this concealment of the obvious there should be a feeling in all artificial construction for beauty of line and contour."[43] Their stance lends itself to a notion of authorship in golf course design that in other sports is more associated with stadiums and spectator accommodations than the playing fields they contain. When someone speaks of Allianz Arena in Munich (opened in 2005), for instance, they are most likely referring to the dazzling stadium structure clad with translucent, inflated cushions made of a high-performance plastic film (ETFE—Ethylene Tetrafluoroethylene) designed by the architecture firm Herzog and de Meuron rather than to attributes of the soccer pitch it encloses. Golf courses reverse this hierarchy. At a prestigious tournament such as the Masters, broadcasters reverently speak in hushed tones the names of the course designers—Alister MacKenzie, Perry Maxwell, Robert Trent Jones, and their successors—while the designers of the clubhouse, temporary seating, and other facilities accommodating the thousands of spectators ("patrons") are anonymous. Writing of such figures with a nod to cognoscenti, Ben Crenshaw, a Masters champion, observes, "Each man had a unique style—brush strokes if you will—making their finished courses all but unmistakable. Who with a well-tutored eye could not identify a [Alistair] MacKenzie bunker, a [Donald] Ross green, a [David] Thomas mound, or a [Albert Warren] Tillinghast hole? Their work bears the stamp of the personalities, beliefs, and opinions—the delicate blending of science and art that adds up to a pleasurable experience on the golf course."[44] The same is said of the work of noted architects and landscape architects. While golf courses, buildings, and landscape architecture can be (and often are) formulaic, these design disciplines offer opportunities for the expression of individualistic approaches.

Wethered and Simpson's charge to designers was fully realized by the British physician-turned-golf-course-architect Alister MacKenzie (1870–1934), whom Crenshaw hailed for his planning of bunkers (they are characterized by their strategic placement in the path of play, their integration with the surroundings, and the shape of their contours). In the long-standing tradition of gentlemen architects and landscape architects, MacKenzie, an avid amateur player, was self-taught and began his design career as a service to the golf clubs to which he belonged in northern England. His practice expanded after World War I. Besides the Augusta National course in Georgia (opened in 1933), site of the Masters Tournament, he was the author of celebrated courses in the United Kingdom, the Americas, Australia, and New Zealand. His other work in the United States includes the Cypress Point course in California (opened 1928), to which I will return. MacKenzie subtly manipulated topographic features and the color and texture of plantings to create puzzles for each hole that challenged players' skill and resourcefulness.

MacKenzie employed, as do golf course architects today, approaches to planning holes that commonly are grouped as the penal, strategic, and heroic schools.[45] The layout of a penal hole presents the player an optimal path from tee to green and penalizes errant shots with ball-eating bunkers (sand traps) and other hazards such as water features. A spectacular example is the 17th hole at the Tournament Players Club at Sawgrass (TPC Sawgrass) in Ponte Vedra Beach, Florida, designed by Pete Dye, which opened in 1980.[46] The distance from tee to the front of the green is 132 yards, not even 1½ times the length of a football field, promising an easily attainable par 3 but for the fact that the green occupies most of a small island, reachable only by lofting the ball across water from the tee (a walkway provides access for players and groundskeepers). Adding to the challenge are a bunker protecting the front of the green and complex slopes on its surface. Any error of distance or direction will send the ball splashing into the drink.

Strategic and heroic holes are similar in that they offer the golfer a choice of several paths to the hole with varying degrees of safety and risk, but heroic holes raise the stakes in dramatic fashion. The 16th hole at Cypress Point is among the most spectacularly daunting of MacKenzie's heroic holes (figure 1.12). Its distance is relatively short, approximately 222 yards, but the most direct path requires the golfer to accurately loft the ball to the small green over an inlet of the Pacific Ocean. The tempting reward for making this shot is a favorable position on the green for completing the hole under par with just one additional shot (par for the hole is three strokes). The risk is a ball deposited in Davy Jones's locker and the mandatory penalty. Although the distance is no deterrent for a skilled golfer, the sight of the crashing waves and the rocky cliff below the green and exposure to a stiff breeze can rattle one's confidence and cause an error-inducing adrenaline spike. Unlike Dye's water-surrounded green at TPC Sawgrass, which must be attacked head on, MacKenzie's design offers the player a choice: attempt

Figure 1.12. 16th hole, Cypress Point golf course, Pebble Beach, California. Designed by Alister MacKenzie, opened 1928. Photograph by Billy Satterfield. Courtesy of Billy Satterfield, Golf Course Gurus.

the heroic shot to the green or take a somewhat less intimidating route that has the attractions of a shorter carry across water and a more forgiving landing area but requires an intermediary shot to reach the green. Achieving par remains possible, but the satisfaction of holing the ball in two shots for a birdie is highly unlikely. Beyond its function as a safer alternative, the option adds a psychological twist that tests the golfer's resolve in choosing a course of action.

In addition to addressing technical considerations such as distance, routing, hazards, plantings, and prevailing breezes, MacKenzie sought to engage the golfer aesthetically. He writes:

> It may at first appear unreasonable that the question of aesthetics should enter into golf course design. However, on deeper analysis it becomes clear that the great courses, and in detail all the famous holes and greens, are fascinating to the golfer by reason of their shape, their situation and the character of their modeling.

> When these elements obey the fundamental laws of balance, of harmony and fine proportion, they give rise to what we call beauty. This excellence of design is more felt than fully realized by the players, but nevertheless it is constantly exercising a subconscious influence upon him and in course of time he grows to admire such a course as works of beauty must be eventually felt and admired.[47]

MacKenzie believed that each hole should have a distinct character to offer golfers a stimulating variety of challenges and pleasures over the course of a round.[48] "The individuality of the holes," the golf course architect Tom Doak elaborates in *The Anatomy of a Golf Course,* "will create a 'flow' to the sequence of play, similar to the musical score of a film, creating a mood for the course."[49] MacKenzie's construction of sequences was masterful. The routing of holes at Cypress Point takes full advantage of the varied topography and vegetation to guide players on a winding journey toward and away from the ocean through woods and open ground.[50] The path from the green of the 15th hole to the tee for the 16th hole, for example, leads through a dense grove of trees that reorients the golfer's view first by constricting it and then suddenly revealing the formidable challenge ahead—an "OMG" moment for many players. The underlying principles of compositional variety, psychological intrigue and surprise, and another of MacKenzie's criteria, the appearance of naturalness, are those of the picturesque, the design aesthetic that has informed the work of landscape architects and architects since the eighteenth century. Cypress Point is a member of a lineage of picturesque landscapes that includes Stowe Gardens in England and New York City's Central Park.

MacKenzie combined his aesthetic predilection for the picturesque with another interest: military camouflage. While serving with the British army as a physician during the Boer War, he observed how the Boer army employed concealed positions to devastating effect in the battle of Colenso (1899) and subsequently advocated for British research and development of camouflage techniques.[51] He pursued the subject after the war alongside his growing practice of golf course design. "The secret of making a well-constructed golf course and a concealed fortification," he later wrote, "is in the imitation of Nature."[52]

World War I occasioned MacKenzie's return to military service, but not as a physician. He enlisted as an officer in the engineering corps and participated in the formation of the British Army School of Camouflage (1916). Interest in his lectures and publications extended to the United States Army.[53] In subsequent reflections on the subject, he noted how experience designing golf courses could be applied to the camouflage of defensive positions: "Golf-course architecture gives one much greater experience in imitating and making the best use of natural features, in increasing one's powers of observation and memorizing the natural features of a country, in simplifying engineering problems, such as drainage, and, above all, in a mental training in strategic problems for devising traps for the enemy than any soldier or engineer could hope to obtain without this experience."[54] MacKenzie observed that traditional practices in both fields had emphasized regularity and the use of stereotyped patterns. As a superior alternative, he pointed to the similar ways "the modern golf architect makes every golfing feature harmonize with nature so as to set a different strategic problem at every hole," and "the Camoufleur (expert on camouflage) makes every defensive position harmonize with the natural features of the landscape so they will escape the observation of the enemy from the ground or from the air."[55]

However much a golf course may harmonize with the natural features of its site, it is, like the settings of the other sports we have considered in this chapter, a construction of distinctive shapes and features that frame the sport's objectives and regulations. There is another aspect to the spatial framing of sports that is external to both the physical properties of the playing field and to the action on it yet profoundly shapes the perception of athletes, officials, and spectators alike. This is the mediation of visual, aural, and text-based sources to which we will now turn.

CHAPTER 2

# MEDIATED SPACE

Walking through my former neighborhood in Pittsburgh, Pennsylvania, on certain fall Sunday afternoons, I could follow the progress of the Steelers' National Football League (NFL) games from radios and televisions heard through open windows. The announcers' commentary was not always intelligible, but there was no mistaking the swings of the game from the piercing exclamations of Myron Cope, the team's longtime color commentator, "Yoi," "Double Yoi," and the superlative, "Triple Yoi!" accompanied by the cheers or groans of my neighbors. If I needed details, porch sitters would happily oblige with the score, time remaining, down-and-distance, and their seasoned assessments of the team's performance. Although I was far from the stadium and unable to see what was happening on the field, the mediation of radio and television broadcasts and my neighbors' commentary allowed me to picture the action in my mind and connect with the rhythm of the game and the community drawn to its performance.

As much as we may participate in sports on the field as players or in the stands as spectators, much of our experience of sporting events is mediated by aural, visual, and text-based sources ranging from a friend's exuberant account of a game ("You should've been there!") to radio and television broadcasts, streaming video on cell phones and tablets, and reports in newspapers and magazines. We integrate these accounts with memories of games that we have seen or heard about and with our other experiences as a player or fan. In addition to providing data points regarding the progress of a game and the performance of individual players and teams, they color our emotional response to the events on the field and the way we experience them spatially. The forms of mediation have expanded greatly in recent years and were particularly prominent during the global coronavirus pandemic of 2020, when most sporting events were held in empty stadiums. But this is not only a twenty-first-century story.

## THE GAME IN A BOX

Mid-nineteenth-century American newspaper publishers seeking to increase circulation found audiences eager to read and willing to pay for accounts of sporting events presented in general-interest dailies and more specialized papers, such as the weekly *Spirit of the Times: A Chronicle of the Turf, Agriculture, Field Sports, Literature and the Stage*, which was launched in New York City in 1831.[1] To its coverage of horse racing, fishing, and cricket, the paper added baseball on July 9, 1853, with a sixty-two-word report of a rain-delayed game between the Gotham and Knickerbocker clubs that had been completed eight days earlier. Accompanying the text was a table listing the players, outs, and runs (the Knickerbockers won 21–12). Early sportswriters soon devised ways of going beyond the reporting of final scores to convey a more vivid sense of how games were played. On June 1, 1875, for example, the *Brooklyn Daily Eagle* published an account, likely written by the pioneering baseball writer Henry Chadwick, of the game played the day before by the New York Mutuals and the Hartford (Connecticut) Dark Blues.

The lede of this brief article of 188 words engaged readers with vivid language and qualitative assessment: "The Mutuals again sustained defeat yesterday, May 31, at the hands of the Hartford Club, simply because they have not yet acquired the art of base running up to the Boston *standard* [referring to the Massachusetts Game as opposed to the Knickerbocker Rules in early baseball], nor are they yet posted *in batting* under the new rules."[2] Describing play, the account reports: "They [Hartford] opened the game in lively style, by getting in two runs, one of which was earned, a dropped fly by [Alfred "Count"] Gedney [the Mutual's left fielder] giving the other. From this time to the close the game was evenly contested, each side scoring one run on a single base hit after the first inning."

Below the text, a detailed box score, a particular interest of Chadwick's, distills the accomplishments of every player statistically, shows the scoring inning by inning, and includes the time of the game (slightly over an hour). The format of the text and box score resemble the game summaries published in newspapers today. Read together, they provide critical data allowing readers to reconstruct the events of the game and prompts for appraising the quality of play. While no special expertise is necessary for a reader to ascertain the game's outcome beyond knowing how to find the final score, visualizing how it was played requires familiarity with the cryptic conventions of box scores and knowledge of the layout of the field, the customary positions of players, and the rules of the game. Much of the reconstruction depends on the reader's imagination to fill in the gaps of the written summary. Newspaper and magazine columnists, book authors, and their counterparts in digital media have the editorial latitude to go beyond the box score and write more expansive and nuanced accounts of the games they cover. In so doing, they can shape their readers' interpretations of the sport like their colleagues on the arts desk, who often enjoy greater cachet.

## I HEARD IT ON THE RADIO

Like newspaper and magazine readers, radio audiences depend on descriptions by others (noteworthy exceptions are the fans in the stands who simultaneously watch the game and listen on portable radios and streaming devices to the broadcasts of their favorite commentators). The first live radio broadcasts of sporting events were produced in 1921 by the station KDKA in Pittsburgh, which aired a boxing match between Pittsburgh native Johnny Ray and Johnny Dundee (April 11: no decision after ten rounds), a baseball game between the Pittsburgh Pirates and the Philadelphia Phillies (August 5: Pirates won 8–5), and a football game between the University of Pittsburgh and West Virginia University (October 8: Pittsburgh won 21–13).[3] The practice spread rapidly across the United States and abroad. In Great Britain, live coverage of soccer began on January 22, 1927, with a broadcast of a match between (London) Arsenal and Sheffield United. Concerned that its audience might have difficulty visualizing the oral account, the BBC's print weekly, *The Radio Times*, published a "listeners' plan" of the Arsenal Football Club Ground in Highbury, London, that divided the pitch into eight numbered zones.[4] During the broadcast, as the play-by-play announcer, Henry Blythe Thornhill Wakelam, described the action, a second announcer, C. A. Lewis, situated it spatially by calling out the zone number to which listeners could refer on their plans. Ungainly as it must have been for listeners sitting in front of their radios to constantly refer to the printed plan, the broadcast, apparently, was well received. The *Times* (London) observed that Wakelam's representation of the game was "notably vivid and impressive." The *Radio Times* continued to provide plans for subsequent broadcasts until the broadcasters and audience learned to envision the action on the field without them (figure 2.1).

Aural media such as radio broadcasts, podcasts, and audio books can inspire a seemingly intimate connection of listeners to announcers. Sportscasters build faithful audiences by inflecting their coverage with a sense of congeniality, as if announcer and listener were sitting side by side in a bar with pints of beer and a shared bowl of popcorn. Although the tone of the broadcast is welcoming, new listeners must master a learning curve to follow along. The pace of play-by-play reporting, particularly for fast-moving games like soccer, hockey, and basketball, allows little opportunity for announcers to explain the rules or to continually specify which player is on which team. A casual listener to a hockey match hears a barrage of player names as the puck is passed, intercepted, and recovered, and, just as they are sorted out, a shift change brings on a new cast of characters. Tuning in to a radio broadcast is a bit like joining a select club whose members enjoy a special language and shared memories. Unlike news announcers, who usually assume unfamiliarity

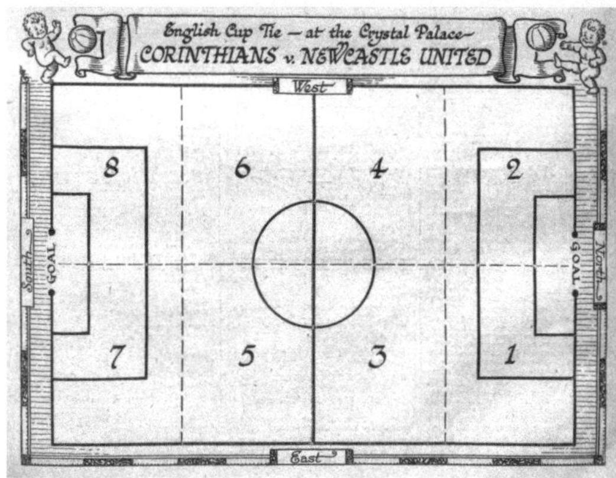


Figure 2.1. Listeners' guide to the Crystal Palace Football Ground, Newcastle United vs. Corinthian F.C., *Radio Times*, January 28, 1927. By special permission from *Radio Times*.

with a story and frame their reporting to bring their audiences up to speed on its key details, radio sportscasters, especially those regarded as "the voice" of specific teams, guide the faithful through practiced rituals.

Experienced listeners don't need a "listeners' plan" to follow a game. They construct their mental images of the action by overlaying the particulars of setting and action communicated by the announcers onto their own memories. To this end, radio sportscasters often provide information that is incidental to the sequence of events but otherwise assists visualization. Craig Way, the longtime play-by-play announcer for the University of Texas at Austin, for instance, begins his coverage of football games with detailed descriptions of the colors and other distinguishing features of the players' uniforms and throughout the game notes the direction of play: "The Longhorns are moving left to right across your radio dial"; "The field goal will be kicked from the near hash mark" (with respect to the location of the broadcast booth).

Today, radio sportscasters regularly report from the site of the game they are covering. This has not always been the case. Minor league baseball teams in the twentieth century, for instance, often did not have the funds to send their announcers on road trips, so broadcasts of away games originated from the hometown studio rather than distant ballparks. A local correspondent would transmit brief running accounts of the game (not unlike social media alerts today) by telegraph, telex, or telephone, and the studio-bound announcer would re-create them for the radio audience. Studio sound effects, including the simulation of the crack of a bat performed with a drumstick and cheers of a crowd played from a phonograph record, added to the verisimilitude of the re-creation, which could lag the events on the field by several minutes (the baseball movie *Bull Durham* vividly portrays this practice). In his memoir, *Play-by-Play: Tales from a Sportscasting Insider*, Bill Mercer describes covering away games in the 1950s for the minor league Muskogee Giants on the station KMUS based in Muskogee, Oklahoma. He and his studio engineer went beyond the use of crowd noises and other generic effects by adding locomotive whistles timed to coincide with the schedule of trains passing by the ballpark.[5]

The extreme brevity of the game summaries and the absence of televised feeds required announcers to embellish their narration with details drawn from their familiarity with players' tendencies and the ebb and flow of the game's competitive tension. Recalling his broadcasts in the early 1960s for KRLD in Dallas, Texas, covering away games played by the minor league Dallas Rangers, Mercer explained how he would portray the action for his listeners:

> Plays on the road were probably more exciting than those at home because I was trying to visualize the circumstances and the difficulty of a play—and to keep the listener entertained. So if there was listed [on the summary], "Jones grounds in a 5–4–3 double play," I would add that Jones hits a sharp grounder down the third-base line, the third baseman backhands the ball, wheels and throws to second for one, relay to first . . . just in time for the double play! Probably it was a routine hopper to third.[6]

The listener's experience of such re-created broadcasts is twice removed from the live action. It is a reconstruction of the announcer's reconstruction.

Whether emanating from the field of play or a studio, radio broadcasts can foster the sense that the announcer is speaking directly to us. We reciprocate by drawing on our personal memories and imagination to transform the announcer's words into mental images of the distant ballpark and the players' positions on the field. This act may inspire that mental state familiar to those who enjoy listening to play-by-play accounts of sports while on long drives or seated on a darkened porch on a summer evening. It's a form of daydreaming grounded by the game's specific location, duration, and outcome, and by the listener's self-awareness. In writing this, I'm reminded of a book that has fascinated generations of architecture students since its appearance in the mid-twentieth century, the phenomenologist Gaston Bachelard's *The Poetics of Space*. Memorably, he writes, "If I were asked to name the chief benefit of the house, I should say: the house shelters daydreaming."[7] For readers who might have thought first of the house protecting its occupants from the elements, a functionalist approach to architecture, the assertion can be unsettling. Aren't daydreams a secondary concern when the roof is leaking? Bachelard likely wouldn't dispute the value of a watertight roof but points to something else by linking the material properties of a house to our imaginative capacity to daydream. Our experience living in a house encompasses the intangible as well as the tangible. Indeed, daydreams depend on our being aware of where we are. Much as the house grounds the daydream for Bachelard, the spatial image of the ballpark conjured in a radio broadcast frames personal reveries that take listeners beyond the circumstances of the game. The challenge for architects designing houses and broadcasters re-creating a distant game is to devise invitations for the inhabitants of the environments they create to daydream.

## I SAW IT ON TELEVISION

Radio broadcasts require audiences to visualize scenes by combining aural cues and associations of memory. Television and streaming video compellingly show an event but mediate our perceptions of space and time with the point of view of the camera and the use of image generators and replay devices. The first live televised sporting event was the 1936 Summer Olympics in Berlin, which was broadcast to special public viewing locations set up in that city and nearby Potsdam.[8] A year later, the BBC inaugurated television coverage of soccer with the presentation of a match in London between Arsenal and Arsenal Reserves.[9] American broadcasters caught up in 1939 when NBC televised a college baseball game between the Columbia University Lions and the Princeton University Tigers to some four hundred pioneering owners of television sets (Princeton won 2–1 in ten innings).[10]

In addition to the technical limitations of early cameras (low resolution, fixed lenses, bulkiness) and receivers (small, low-resolution screens), early television coverage of baseball faced challenges that were inherent in the game's spatial qualities. Baseball has a less predictable directional flow than football and soccer, which lend themselves to coverage by a camera panning across the length of the field. Ballparks are large, the infield and outfield have very different configurations, and the action can be dispersed. At the same time the pitcher and batter duel over control of the strike zone, a base runner may threaten to steal a base and the infielders and outfielders may adjust their defensive alignments. When the batter makes contact with the ball, it may be hit softly as an infield bunt dribbling along the third-base line, hammered as a towering home run into the center-field bleachers, or launched out of play above and behind the catcher. Spectators in the stands rely on their peripheral vision to follow this multifarious activity. The view on a television screen is limited by the camera lens. A wide-angle shot can show the entire field but loses detail on small screens. Closeups provide clarity but can miss important action occurring outside the frame.

When regular televised presentations of Major League Baseball games became widespread after World War II, broadcasters typically employed two cameras placed at different vantage points behind home plate. By 1951, the station WOR had expanded its setup for Brooklyn Dodgers games at Ebbets Field to five cameras: one in the press box above and behind home plate and two pairs of cameras situated high and low along the first- and third-base lines. Four years later, the pioneering sports television director Harry Coyle introduced a sixth, center field camera for CBS's coverage of the All-Star Game. It completed the base configuration augmented today by additional cameras dedicated to coverage of individual players and specific areas of the field. As James R. Walker and Robert Bellamy Jr. describe in their book *Center Field Shot: A History of Baseball on Television*, broadcasters have continually increased the number of cameras and other recording devices, such as on-field microphones, to provide their audiences with ever-closer views of the game. Today, the cut-ins, fades, and other details of players' hairstyles are part of the play-by-play commentary alongside analysis of pitch selection and batting style. For the television broadcast of the 2023 World Series, Fox Sports employed fifty-two cameras, including one mounted on the plate umpire's mask, and more than one hundred microphones positioned around the field for the games played at Globe Life Field in Arlington, Texas, and Chase Field in Phoenix, Arizona.[11]

What the viewer sees of the multitude of images and sounds captured by these devices is determined by the broadcast director, who makes selections intended to portray the flow of the game compellingly.[12] The director's choices shape the way viewers perceive it spatially. Coyle's shot selection in the days before the introduction of the center-field camera is evident in the fortuitously surviving kinescope of NBC's coverage of Game 7 of the 1952 World Series between the Yankees and the (Brooklyn) Dodgers (the Yankees took the title with a 4–2 win).[13] For Jackie Robinson's turn at the plate for the Dodgers in the bottom of the first inning, Coyle set the scene with an establishing shot from a vantage point behind and above home plate (figure 2.2). The camera operator tightly framed the image to include the pitcher, Eddie Lopat, at the top of the screen, and the batter, catcher, and umpire at the bottom. Only the segments of the baselines radiating from home plate suggest the expanse of the field. The high-view angle tips the appearance of the visual plane of the field upward and flattens the depth of

Figure 2.2. Kinescope recording screenshot showing Jackie Robinson batting, Eddie Lopat pitching, and Pee Wee Reese leading off first base, Game 7, 1952 World Series. www.youtube.com/watch?v=hqZnPQnxO9U. Courtesy of MLB.

the scene. Robinson's at bat was not the only action occurring on the field. His teammate, Pee Wee Reese, was on first base attempting to distract the pitcher's attention with threats to steal second base. Since this game of cat and mouse was outside the frame of the establishing shot, Coyle covered it by superimposing a shot from a camera on the first-base line, which introduced a ghostly image of Reese and first baseman Johnny Mize on the screen. Robinson hit the ball on the first pitch, and Coyle tracked its flight into deep left field and the glove of Yankee outfielder Gene Woodling with a panning view from the home plate camera and a cut to a telephoto shot from above the first-base line.

The introduction of the center-field camera reoriented the way viewers see the field. Instead of facing the pitcher from above home plate, the vantage point of the establishing shot is behind the pitcher's shoulder and facing the batter. It allows viewers to focus on the vertical plane of the strike zone. Coyle had honed this convention by the time he covered Bill Mazeroski's celebrated, bottom-of-the-ninth-inning home run (dubbed the "shot heard 'round the world") that clinched the 1960 World

Series for the Pittsburgh Pirates over the Yankees.[14] The low center-field camera position at Pittsburgh's Forbes Field and the use of a telephoto lens gives viewers a foreshortened perspective, as if watching Mazeroski's at bat from second base. The pitcher and batter fill the frame of the shot. After the bat launched the ball, Coyle held the center-field camera's shot for a moment to capture Mazeroski's first steps toward first base and then flipped the point of view by cutting to a high-angle camera that followed the flight of the ball over the outfield wall.

The television director's artful selection of shots guides viewers through a game by capturing its pace and articulating a narrative structure. Joe Aceti, renowned for his work at ABC, CBS, and Fox from the late 1960s to his retirement in 2001, described shot selection in terms of sequencing.[15] In baseball, rather than covering the interval between pitches from a stationary position, he would dramatize what was to come by presenting viewers with a sequence of close-up and medium shots showing the catcher looking to the dugout for instructions, the manager's hand signals, the third-base coach signaling the batter or base runners, the batter preparing his stance, the catcher signing the recommended pitch, the pitcher's acceptance or dismissal of the signs, and, finally, the throw. Shot by shot, the viewers would be led into a story building on unspoken questions prompted by the visual cues. Will the manager give the base runner the steal sign? What pitch will the catcher call, and will the pitcher agree? Will the batter take the pitch hoping that it will be out of the strike zone, take a full swing, or bunt? The director can shape the pacing of the story by the timing of the cuts, lingering on a close-up as a pitcher reads the catcher's signs or making quick jump cuts to follow communication between players and coaches.

When handled well, the rhythm of the cutting complements the athlete's movement. Aceti enjoyed directing broadcasts of figure skating competitions, for which he would compose shots and time cuts in accordance with the choreography and musical accompaniment. In an interview with the visual media scholar Lawrence Mullen, he recounted demonstrating how to shape the presentation of a skater's routine to a network executive:

> Here's what you have to do, tell camera two to widen out, frame her [the skater] on the left, tell [camera] three to pan right—you have to make the camera shots different—different in size, different angles, and so forth. . . . You have to cut on the music, but not incorrectly like when the skater is jumping in the air. You never cut anything when it is in the air. You don't cut in the middle of a jump. . . . You never want to cut with anything in the air, a baseball, a basketball, a football. It's not good television. You have to keep screen direction all the time and you should not over-cut.[16]

Aceti's cautions regarding cutting in the middle of a jump or the flight of a ball, over-cutting, and the importance of screen direction pertain to the director's obligation to help the viewer maintain a coherent spatial image much in the same way a radio sportscaster refers to play moving from left to right across the radio dial.

The conventions of camera angles and shot sequences employed in television coverage of sporting events condition viewers' expectations of how to follow a game visually. Fans raised on a diet of televised baseball, for example, can grasp a game's flow on a muted screen across a room from the shot sequence: when the director cuts to the center-field camera, a pitch, most likely, will follow. The director's view and interpretation of the game become ours.

In his book *Fields in Vision: Television Sport and Cultural Transformation*, the scholar of mass culture Garry Whannel describes television broadcasts of sporting events with respect to an aesthetic continuum that ranges from an objective—or in his terms, realist—presentation at one end and entertainment at the other.[17] An example of the former is the subscription-based All-22 Coaches Film coverage offered by the NFL, which provides fixed views of the entire field from high vantage points (sideline and end zone). Approximating the experience of a spectator in the nosebleed seats, it sacrifices detail for a view of the whole. As in the stadium, the viewer can focus freely on whatever aspect of a play is of most interest—the blocking schemes of the offensive line, for instance—while maintaining peripheral awareness of the action of the other players.

Most television broadcasts of sports operate more on the entertainment side of Whannel's scale, seeking to hold viewers' attention by emphasizing so-called pleasure points that are visually stimulating and emotionally engaging.[18] While maintaining some aspects of the objective viewpoint—most evidently in the use of wide-angle establishing shots at the beginning of a sequence of play—directors highlight pleasure points with medium and close-up shots that maximize the action visible on our screens. In the confines of this viewing window, the sociologist Tim Dant notes, we perceive figures in motion as in a state of becoming, an unfolding story that draws our curiosity about the outcome.[19] Directors frame and sequence shots to heighten the inherent drama and hold the attention of viewers by inviting them to identify with the players. Emerging video technologies take this practice another step by employing camera shots that approximate the point of view of individual players. Familiar in television broadcasts of American football are the cable-suspended SkyCam systems that swoop over the field as low as twelve feet above the heads of players. Increasingly, first-person views are being introduced by cameras affixed to the bodies of players and officials. The action is vivid, but the view is limited. While the player or official on the field composes the scene through subtle, rapid eye movement, the remote viewer is subject to the constraints of the camera's position and lens settings.

Skilled television directors strike a balance between fine-grained details and the whole in their broadcasts, but the mediated experience they present has different spatial qualities than those viewers encounter on the field, in the stands, or when watching whole-field coverage. Medium and close-up shots put us amid the action but fracture our perception of the continuity of the physical space the players occupy because they trade off context for isolated detail. When we witness the interval between pitches at a baseball game from the stands, we can follow the interactions of coaches and players while maintaining peripheral awareness of the entire field of play and the location of the beer vendor. On the screen, our view is much narrower. The shot sequencing may be in real time, but it decomposes and reframes the scene, even taking us away from the field of play with panoramic aerial shots, glimpses of local life (often food related, especially deep-fried), and images of other fans in the stands or watching the broadcast remotely.

## LET'S GO TO THE REPLAY

Alongside the fragmentation of space, television broadcasts fragment and reorder time. Viewers watching the fourth quarter of CBS's coverage of the annual Army-Navy football game on December 7, 1963, saw Army quarterback Rollie Stichweh plunge across the goal line on a 1-yard run to pull the Cadets within a touchdown of the favored Midshipmen. Moments later, they saw him do it again. Had Army somehow seized the lead in a blink of an eye? Play-by-play announcer Lindsey Nelson emphatically assured startled viewers that they had not missed anything: "This is not live! Ladies and gentlemen, Army did not score again." Instead, they had witnessed the first instant replay broadcast in the United States. After a succession of glitches earlier in the game, CBS director Tony Verna and his crew had managed to quickly retrieve broadcast-quality images from a 1,200-pound videotape machine harnessed to a camera dedicated to covering the quarterbacks. Verna's demonstration paved the way for acceptance of recently introduced videotape technology that offered more rapidly accessible and cost-effective replays than those produced with kinescope film, which the Canadian Broadcasting Corporation producer George Retzlaff had introduced in 1955 for "Hockey Night in Canada."[20] These first replays were shown at full speed, but over the decade of the 1960s, broadcast crews led by Verna, Coyle, and other innovators, including the ABC producer Roone Arledge, mastered the use of slow motion and stop-action techniques that are now ubiquitous in sports broadcasts.

Replays concentrate engaging moments of play—Whannel's pleasure points—by situating viewers in spatial and temporal frames different from those experienced on the field or in the stands. Taken to an extreme, as with video compilations of "greatest plays," games may be reduced to strings of highlights divorced from their contexts. This strategy for depicting events, which is not limited to sports, has attracted the attention of television theorists. In an influential essay, the film and television studies scholar Jane Feuer discusses what she terms an ideology of liveness, in which television operates on a premise of the flow and continuity of the live but is more accurately described as "a collage of film, video and 'live,' all interwoven into a complex and altered time scheme."[21] Using coverage of the Winter Olympics as an example, she observes how broadcasters segment and fragment the competitive events to create entertaining narratives of athletes' aspirations. Long-distance Nordic cross-country races and other events not well suited for representation on the screen because of lengthy duration, lack of visual drama, immense venues, or limited viewer interest are enlivened by cross-cutting camera angles and isolating particularly exciting moments, such as a crowd of skiers negotiating a squeeze point on the trail or the final sprint to the finish line.[22]

The most compelling moments are distilled as replays and are shown repeatedly. Building on Feuer's theory of liveness and the philosopher Henri Bergson's foundational studies of perception and memory published at the end of the nineteenth century, the media scholar Christopher Hanson has considered our response to seeing the same clips again and again.[23]

The replay, he explains, is an event with its own properties of form, content, and duration that become independent of their context on the field. Although the replay does not change as it loops, no viewing experience is the same because of the spectator's ever-changing personal circumstances and cumulative memory. Through repeated viewings, replays can take on their own significance apart from the game of which they are but a fragment.

On November 23, 2014, the New York Giants quarterback Eli Manning threw a long pass downfield to the rookie receiver Odell Beckham Jr., who was racing along the sideline while trying to disentangle himself from the hands of Dallas

Cowboys cornerback Brandon Carr. Two yards from the goal line, Beckham stretched and snared the ball with one hand just before it would have sailed out of bounds (figure 2.3). Amid a shower of referees' yellow penalty flags thrown in response to Carr's interference before the catch, Beckham clutched the ball to his chest and tumbled into the endzone for a touchdown. The sequence, which NBC covered with a panning shot from a high vantage point on the opposite side of the field, occurs in a blur lasting about three seconds from the moment when the ball leaves Manning's hand to Beckham's score. The catch itself flashes by in less than one second and is so difficult to follow in the wide-angle shot that recognition of its success follows more from the sideline official's upraised arms indicating a touchdown than the blur of what had transpired. As Beckham and his teammates celebrated in real time, NBC's director explicated the achievement with a series of slow-motion replays from near-side, far-side, and end-zone cameras. The image of Beckham's backward reach with the ball snagged by his fingertips recorded in these shots and in the frames captured by nearby

Figure 2.3. One-handed touchdown catch by Odell Beckham Jr., New York Giants vs. Dallas Cowboys, November 23, 2014. Cal Sport Media/Alamy.

still photographers was distributed widely and quickly became a popular internet meme.

The replays isolate the play from the surrounding action as a pleasure point by framing Beckham and Carr tightly. The telephoto camera lenses further concentrate the scene by compressing the depth of field. The slow-motion movement of receiver and defender against the background of the turf and the nearly static crowd standing along the sideline illustrates Dant's analysis of how figures in motion spark our curiosity as an unfolding drama. Will Beckham secure the ball? Will Carr succeed in a final, desperate attempt to break up the play?

Their performance is framed visually by the field markings and conceptually by the rules of the game. The Giants designed the play to utilize the properties of the sideline as an edge that limited Beckham's exposure to Carr and other defenders. The rules balanced this advantage by requiring Beckham to remain in bounds while running his route and completing the catch. Slow-motion recordings, as the philosophers of sport David Best and John Holt have observed, provide opportunities for aesthetic appreciation of the grace of athletic movement.[24] The image of Beckham's outstretched posture inspired the author of at least one internet meme to paste it into a photo of a line of ballet dancers.

The clips replaying the entire play, which years later are still readily available on YouTube and other digital platforms, possess a dramatic arc beginning with the real-time, wide-angle shot of quarterback Manning positioning himself for the pass as Beckham fends off Carr during his run along the sideline followed by a slow-motion montage of the catch and subsequent celebration. As entertainment, many viewers find it more memorable and appealing for repeated viewing than the full game, which the Giants went on to lose 31–28 in one more episode of a frustrating season. It exemplifies Whannel's observation that "with their ability to offer a series of rapidly changing perspectives, television has invented, in effect, an original form of drama. In particular, slow-motion replay offers entirely new events outside of real time and space. Slow-motion replay not only alters our perceptions of the action it reviews, but also establishes our expectations."[25] Just as television-watching baseball fans have been conditioned to follow an at bat through a standard sequence of shots that frame the duel between batter and pitcher in a specific way, the prevalence of replays imposes a hierarchy onto the action on the field. Television and live-stream-video audiences repeatedly see events selected by the television director forward and backward and from multiple angles with cuts jumped according to familiar rhythms. So do fans in the stands and players and officials on the field.

## YOU MAKE THE CALL! JUMBOTRONS AND VIDEO REVIEW

The first stadium replays in the United States were shown on the scoreboard at Arrowhead Stadium, home of the NFL's Kansas City (Missouri) Chiefs, in 1972. Three years later, the Louisiana Superdome (now Caesars Superdome) followed suit.[26] Today, mammoth video displays are must-have features in professional and college sports venues. Mercedes-Benz Stadium in Atlanta, which opened in 2017 as the home of the Atlanta Falcons (NFL) and the Atlanta United FC (Major League Soccer, MLS), boasts a 63,000-square-foot, 58-foot-high display that forms a halo around the interior of the stadium high above the field.

The availability of instant replays to spectators and players in the stadium, as well as to viewers watching remotely, has posed challenges for game officials. Blown or missed calls, replayed in slow motion from a variety of camera angles, are visible to all. Officials ignoring this evidence (often by rule) miss opportunities to fulfill their obligation to administer the game fairly and accurately and risk losing credibility with fans and players.[27] Incorporating replays in the deliberative process adds a tool for maintaining the integrity of the game. The NFL introduced limited use of replays by officials in 1986, and other sports have followed suit since.

FIFA, the international association governing soccer, instituted for the 2018 World Cup a system of reviews managed by a new position—video assistant referees (VAR). Reviews are limited to prescribed circumstances including goals, certain penalties—among them offside violations—and cases of mistaken identity in awarding yellow and red cards. They may be initiated by the referee on the field or the VAR who leads a team of video assistants monitoring video feeds of the game. Communicating with the VAR by wireless headsets, the referee may act on information shared verbally or consult a sideline video display before making a final decision. As with replay reviews in other sports, the stoppage of play fractures the flow of the game and shifts attention from the realm of players and officials on the field to the mediating technology. The review is an administrative part of the game, yet temporally and visually external to the flow of action on the field. It is an event with its own structure and duration introducing a new level of dramatic tension for spectators watching the looping video of replay camera shots and the officials pondering their decision. Officials do not simply discuss what they thought they saw; they can repeatedly view in high definition what had passed in a blur. The replay angles and slow-motion imagery frame points of view not readily observable in real time, revealing details such as a minute offside infraction in soccer, the edge of an NFL receiver's shoe kissing the chalk during a run along the sideline, or whether a soccer ball or hockey puck entered the goal.

In most sports, reviews of infractions are initiated by officials or coaches and must be resolved before play continues, but in golf, a review can be initiated by a fan watching a television broadcast thousands of miles away from the course, and outcomes may not be determined until after a match has ended. The rules of the United States Golf Association allow any witness to report infractions overlooked by players and course officials. Bill Pennington and Karen Crouse examined this practice for the *New York Times* following an incident at the 2013 Masters Tournament when a fan watching on television sent a text message to officials reporting that superstar Tiger Woods had not followed the correct procedure for putting a new ball in play after an errant shot into a pond at the fifteenth hole.[28] The next day, the tournament rules committee assessed a two-stroke penalty that placed Woods five strokes behind the leader, a setback he was not able to overcome (Adam Scott won the tournament). Pennington and Crouse found that such involvement by fans following PGA (Professional Golfers' Association of America) tournaments on television was not uncommon and traced its history at least twenty-five years to the 1987 San Diego Open (now the Farmers Insurance Open), when multiple television viewers cried foul after Craig Stadler made the error of kneeling on a towel to make a shot under a tree. This act of sartorial fastidiousness (he was trying to keep his pants clean) breached the prohibition of "building a stance," or altering the site to better position a shot. Stadler did not report the violation. A day later he was disqualified from the tournament for signing an inaccurate scorecard. Had his posted score been upheld, he would have taken third place (George Burns won the tournament).

The video replays and livestreams shown on stadium screens are not watched only by spectators. Players make use of them as well. During American football games, ball carriers running downfield occasionally can be spotted looking up at the live feed on the video screen to locate pursuers. During the 2024 Super Bowl, Kansas City Chiefs quarterback Patrick Mahomes, sprawled on the ground facing away from the play, tracked his pass on the big screen. Less noticeably, wide receivers may use it to check alignments, and blockers may sneak peeks to observe defensive shifts. As a matter of perception, these actions require a complex integration of inputs. While in motion and confronting agile opponents, players must quickly shift focus to the distant screen, locate themselves in the image, and embody that information. This does not always work smoothly. Tiki Barber, a former running back for the New York Giants, explained, "You will sometimes see I am running straight ahead, and I will start to reach my hand out before I am getting tackled. I know he [the opponent] is coming, and sometimes [the video image] messes me up. Sometimes I will swing, and I will miss because I am seeing it, but he really is not there yet."[29] Barber's description of cognitive dissonance exemplifies the psychologist Mihaly Csikszentmihalyi's notion of psychic entropy, whereby an athlete's sense of flow is disrupted by the information on the screen.[30] Athletes must master new perceptual skills to embody such inputs seamlessly.

Whenever there is a pause in the action, players on the field and sidelines can be seen looking up to watch the replay on the stadium video screen, becoming spectators of their own performance. They may take advantage of replays to adjust technique and tactics (this also is done using tablets and other devices displaying video recorded for coaching purposes) or simply for entertainment. The former Atlanta Falcons quarterback Michael Vick has described turning to the big screen after throwing an incomplete pass: "[I looked] just to see my mechanics or what I did that was wrong. But most of the time [it was] to look at myself, and make sure that I'm looking good in my uniform."[31] For Vick and many other athletes, the video is an instrument of reflection for improving performance and cultivating a particular image to fans and sponsors. A familiar example of the latter is the celebrations after touchdowns in American football that feature individual signature moves, choreographed group dance steps, and poses by players who often are viewing their performances in real time on end-zone video screens.

Players, coaches, and team officials also have experimented with ways to use the video displays of their home stadiums to influence the outcome of games. In football, for example, video display operators may quickly run replays favoring certain views intended to encourage the referees to make a favorable decision. Less subtly, in 2020, the video operator at Oklahoma State University's Boone Pickens Stadium sought to upset the concentration of the University of Texas's field goal kicker by playing on the video screen behind the goal post a pattern of yellow vertical lines that were the same color as the uprights.[32] The virtual space of the screen was intended to intrude on the real space and perception of the kicker. The effort was for naught. The kick was good.

Another example of a team using live video to gain a competitive edge during games is the notorious and illicit case of the Houston Astros' sign-stealing scheme conducted over several seasons until brought to a halt by MLB in January 2020.[33]

Taking advantage of the leisurely pace between pitches and the broadcast feed of the centerfield camera, the team monitored the opposing catchers' signs indicating the type of pitch to be thrown to the Astros' batter. The selection would be relayed from the video station to the Astros' dugout by a runner or a text message. A player in the dugout would then bang on a trash can to alert the batter—one or two whacks for a curveball or another off-speed pitch, none for a fastball. In 2019, the Astros allegedly upgraded this final step to the more high-tech solution of equipping the batter with a buzzer worn under his jersey, although this was never proven. Sign stealing is a time-honored tradition in baseball, but while it is permissible for a base runner to spy on the opposing catcher and signal the pitch selection to his teammate at bat, it is illegal to augment what players and coaches can see from their positions in the field and dugout. The Astros drew the ire of the broader baseball community by outsourcing their espionage. Their use of video as a tactical aid unilaterally altered the parameters of the game's spatial frame.

## THE VIDEO MIRROR

A more positive application of photographic and videographic mediation can be found in sports for which performance style has high value. The architectural historian and theorist Iain Borden examines this phenomenon at length in *Skateboarding, Space and the City*. "The skateboarder's undertaking of a move," he observes, "is a complex intersection of lived experience and mechanically reproduced imagery, in which the latter acts as a kind of mirror, not only reflecting the subject's image back to herself or himself but also extending a repetition/symmetry immanent to the body into the space; the mechanical image projects the skater both back to herself and out to others."[34]

Skateboarders learn their sport by watching others at skateparks and by studying photographs in magazines, videos posted on YouTube and other social media platforms, and video clips and photos they exchange personally. The object of the skater's study goes beyond the technique required to execute a move. "If a rider looks good, if he has style," the professional skateboarder Steve Caballero states in a 1989 interview in the skateboarding magazine *Thrasher*, "his tricks are going to look all the more healthy for it. And he'll feel a lot better . . . a more complete skater."[35] Borden explains that skateboarders construct an identity for themselves with respect to the number, difficulty, and smoothness of the moves in their repertoires. They refine their tricks through intense comparative study of images of other skaters performing the same or similar moves and of their own performances in the same way dancers monitor their form by facing a wall of mirrors in a studio. In turn, skaters disseminate their moves as images among the skateboarding community. "The move," Borden notes, "is the unit of exchange between skaters."[36]

Borden's point about mechanically reproduced imagery in the form of photographs and videos "extending a repetition/symmetry immanent to the body into space," refers to mediated expression of the "delicate relation between body, board, terrain and gravitational force" that is at the heart of skateboarding.[37] This moment of grace, fleeting in real time, is captured in the photograph or video and highlighted by the photographer's framing of the image, which, for instance, may employ a low vantage point to emphasize the skateboarder's separation from the ground or draw the viewer into the scene with the perspective of a wide-angle lens.[38]

## STEP INTO AUGMENTED REALITY

"Philosophically," the ethicist and scholar of emerging technologies Andy Miah writes in *Sport 2.0: Transforming Sports for a Digital World*, "immersion into an alternate reality is an appealing goal for users, since the prospect invites us to consider, and subsequently experience, what it is like to inhabit another person's life—to live as if one is somebody else."[39] Traditional televisual broadcasts shape sporting events for a mass audience by employing teams of producers, directors, and commentators who determine the point of view and interpret the action on the field. Until recently, fans unsatisfied by this coverage have had few options to customize this degree of mediation apart from workarounds such as listening to a favorite announcer on the radio while watching the muted television broadcast and enduring asynchronous transmission delays. Spurred by the popularity of first-person video games and e-sports, the technological advances of ever-smaller digital cameras, increased computing power, and expanded digital bandwidth, broadcasters and developers of hardware and software are rapidly devising media platforms that allow remote viewers to select what they want to see and hear from a menu of video and audio streams. These include options for switching among a variety of camera positions located around the playing field and following certain players equipped with body cameras.[40] Virtual reality goggles that isolate viewers from their surroundings make the experience even more immersive.

The closer the action of a sporting event, however, the faster it appears. Video from body cameras lacks the context and smoothness of the multifaceted perception of our direct, physical experience and can be disorienting. "The project of virtual reality," Miah observes, "requires us to acknowledge that our sensory capacities may also need modification in order for them to deliver the kind of immersive experience we seek."[41] He points to the value of slow motion as a device to help us adjust the pace and complexity of the action to levels that can be comprehended and imagined on our own terms.

Another aid is the addition of interpretive data, which traditionally has been the role of radio and television commentators. Television broadcasters and streaming video producers often complement aural descriptions with displays of text and other graphics. In the early days of televised baseball, before the development of graphics generators, directors would superimpose a shot of a printed name card on a shot of a batter or, even more simply, focus a camera on the stadium scoreboard and allow viewers to read the game statistics and updates on games being played elsewhere.[42] In 1998, ESPN introduced the virtual first-down line in its coverage of NFL games.[43] Appearing on the screen as part of the field, except that it mysteriously relocates with each set of downs, the line is a superimposed graphic generated by an intricate system developed by Sportvision that integrates digital modeling of the field, chromakeying superimposed images, and correcting distortions of camera angles. The device provides television viewers with a much clearer image of the distance a team must cover to maintain possession of the ball than that available to spectators in the stands, who must mentally correlate the position of the ball with the location of the down markers on the sideline. Today, the same technology generates additional graphics highlighting information such as the distance a team must advance to be within the field goal kicker's effective range and the probability of success from a given point.

For its coverage of baseball, ESPN began superimposing an outline of the strike zone on its live shots of batters in 2015. The sharply rendered rectangle floating above home plate provides viewers with a seemingly precise, mechanistically authoritative standard for locating pitches as balls or strikes, but in so doing, it creates an epistemological gap between the way television audiences and the players, umpires, and spectators in the ballpark view the game. For the television viewer, the strike zone is an object appearing without qualification. On the screen, the pitched ball passes either outside or inside the box, which in the standard shot is depicted as a rectangle coincident with the front edge of home plate (replays often employ oblique views that facilitate volumetric representations). The umpire, on the other hand, and others in the stadium, mentally construct the zone as a three-dimensional volume correlating the measurements of the plate and the stance of the batter. A pitch with a late-breaking curve may miss the front plane of the strike zone but nip a back corner for a backdoor strike.[44] Umpires inevitably vary in the way they envision the edges of the zone—the strike zone of some umpires is more generous than that of others—but if the calls are consistent, batters for the most part tend to temper objections and adjust their swings accordingly. Long considered part of the game, allowance for this elasticity now is being reconsidered with the use of automated strike zones, which discriminate strikes and balls according to the parameters of the enabling hardware and software and alert the umpire accordingly.[45]

Baseball is not the only sport to incorporate automated digital mediation in game management. Professional cricket leagues pioneered the use of optical, acoustic, and even infrared devices to track ball trajectories and detect the slightest contact with the bat or the batter's body.[46] The Hawk-Eye optical ball-tracking system first introduced to cricket in 2001 has been adapted to determine line calls in tennis (figure 2.4). Initially used as an aid to replay officials, in recent years it has increasingly been employed in real time, replacing human line judges. In the name of improving objectivity and accuracy, these systems supplement the spatial perception of players and officials with information derived externally.

The global coronavirus pandemic that began in 2020 brought heightened attention to the way televisual and audio technologies mediate spectators' experience of sports.[47] As professional sports organizations resumed play in stadiums and arenas devoid of spectators, or nearly so, league administrators and their broadcast partners worried that the absence of the

Figure 2.4. Andy Murray watches a Hawk-Eye electronic line call, Wimbledon Championships, July 5, 2015. PA Images/Alamy.

familiar cheers and background murmur of fans in the seats would diminish the engagement of television, radio, and live-stream audiences. There was concern, as well, for the unknown effect the silent stadiums would have on the performance of players who no longer could find inspiration in the cheers or boos of the crowd.

The situation underscored the role of sound in the architecture of sports. While sight commonly is given precedence, sound also contributes to spatial perception. We respond both to the sources of sounds and to the way sounds resonate in a landscape or building. "Hearing structures and articulates the experience and understanding of space," writes the architect Juhani Pallasmaa in *The Eyes of the Skin: Architecture and the Senses*, a call for greater recognition that we experience architecture as physically embodied beings. I will return to this notion with respect to spatial practices in sports in chapter 3. Continuing his discussion of hearing, Pallasmaa notes how removing the soundtrack from a film disrupts the depth ("plasticity" is his word), continuity, and life of a scene.[48] Similarly, in a building, the resonance of voices in a room, the taps of approaching footsteps, and the hum of a refrigerator contribute to our spatial awareness, even if not intentionally designed by the architect. Changes to the background sounds of a building can be as unsettling as the loss of a film soundtrack. My wife, a former curator of education at Fallingwater, the house designed by Frank Lloyd Wright over a waterfall in western Pennsylvania, tells of a cold winter day when the staff working inside noticed something amiss. For a while, they couldn't account for it until someone realized that the falls had frozen. The absence of the sound of flowing water disrupted a signature element of the experience of being in the house.

The acoustic environment of sporting events includes the chatter and cheers of spectators and the sounds of play. The roar of the crowd at once reflects and heightens a collective sense of excitement among fans and players. Architects and operators of stadiums and arenas intent on enhancing the spectacle of the game-day experience for those in the stands shape the acoustical environment with sound-focusing layouts of seating and roof shapes, reflective materials, and powerful sound systems.[49] The sounds of play orient participants to the action. Assistant referees in soccer, for instance, listen for the thunk of a kick in one area of the field while watching the positioning of players in another to determine an offside infraction. Television producers mediate these sounds for their viewers by, for example, assigning technicians to follow play from the sidelines with parabolic microphones aimed to capture the sounds of football quarterbacks' snap counts and the impact of colliding bodies.

Broadcasters on occasion take creative license in enhancing the acoustic setting. Radio announcers covering baseball games from their home studios don't have a monopoly on such invention. CBS television, for instance, has surreptitiously embellished the bucolic images of golf tournaments by adding prerecorded birdsong.[50] During the COVID-19 pandemic, baseball in Korea and soccer in Europe were among the first sports to proceed with their seasons and paved the way for introducing recordings of fan noise into the broadcast feeds and stadiums. The practice quickly became widespread as additional sports began play in stadiums and arenas devoid of fans. It required more than cueing up tracks of generic crowd sounds. Producers sought to achieve a degree of authenticity by composing the virtual soundscapes with clips of past games played before a team's home crowd. In this effort, the audio libraries compiled by Electronic Arts for its computer sports games were valuable resources. Technicians familiar with the typical behavior of a team's home crowd would adjust the selection and volume of the recorded fan sounds as plays unfolded in real time. Such curation imposes the producers' values on the scene. MLB, for instance, banned clips of booing or other expressions of negativity apart from groans accompanying situations such as a long fly ball falling foul rather than staying in bounds for a home run.[51]

Highly mediated sporting events present spectators with a very different experience from that of fans in the stands. Television and streaming video go beyond offering a simple window onto the playing field to present viewers with information displays that statistically quantify the physical action and overlay the game at hand with accounts and images of sporting events unfolding elsewhere. Are these framing devices too far removed from the physical essence of sports? This might be so if we mistake the human competitors for algorithms, but augmented reality remains grounded in an event occurring in a specific time and place. Acknowledging the differences, Miah accepts both as meaningful experiences: "Mediated and even live first-person forms of spectating are all creative, synthetic human constructions, no single version being able to claim greater proximity to the true experience, or the way sport really is, than any other."[52] In the next chapter, we'll take a closer look at the experiential and performative aspects of playing and watching sports.

CHAPTER 3

# LABORATORIES OF SPATIAL INVENTION

A Major League Baseball game begins when the umpire commands, "Play ball!" A hockey match begins with an official dropping the puck between the sticks of two opposing players. These acts do more than the practical task of getting a game underway. They also mark the transformation of the playing field, whether a worn playground or a championship stadium, from a place of memories and anticipation to a discrete social space governed by special rules of behavior and time measurement. Some sports mark the transition from the ordinary to the extraordinary with additional rituals. At major international tournaments, New Zealand's national rugby teams, the All Blacks and Black Ferns, perform the chants and choreographed movements of Maori *haka* as expressions of cultural identity and commitment (figure 3.1).[1] More elaborate, still, are the rituals in Japan before each Grand Sumo bout symbolizing the purification of the ring (the *dohyō*) and the wrestlers.

When play ends, the social space dissolves and the rules of ordinary behavior resume. Players, coaches, support staff, and family members mingle on the field, seeking out friends on the opposing team and acknowledging the conclusion of the competition. Some sports formalize this transition. Hockey has a long-standing practice of postgame handshake lines. Grand Sumo ends each day of a tournament with the bow-twirling ceremony (*yumitori-shiki*) in which a wrestler performs a series of movements with a bamboo bow to banish malevolent spirits from the *dohyō*. Less formal traditions include competitors joining together for a postgame drink, or two, at a nearby bar—the 19th hole of golf.

Figure 3.1. New Zealand Black Ferns perform a *haka* before their match vs. Australia Wallaroos, 2021 Women's Rugby League World Cup Final, Manchester, UK, November 19, 2022. Andrew Rowland/PRIME Media Images/Alamy.

In the previous chapters, I described properties of the frames of sports—the playing fields—and how print, broadcast, and digital media represent them. Frames define boundaries separating players and spectators and regulate aspects of play. They can impose direction on movement, but the goals and means constituting the sports they serve are defined by the rules of competition. In this chapter, I consider spatial invention in athletic performance between the starting and ending whistles. My scope goes beyond the strategic and tactical inventions that dominate sports talk. I'll begin with a closer look at the activation of a field, court, or other competition venue as an extraordinary social space. Within this realm, players and coaches devise approaches to exploit the opportunities afforded by the frame and the rules of the game. The field of play becomes a laboratory of spatial invention. From the seeming objectivity of plays diagrammed on a coach's whiteboard, I'll turn to the subjective spatial experience of players and spectators shaped by point of view, memory, and aspiration. This topic links the spatial practices of sports with other arenas of spatial invention through the philosophical concept of aesthetic engagement—being fully present in the moment. In a discussion on dance that pertains equally to sports, the philosopher Arnold Berleant writes, "Movement in dance creates a presentational realm in which the body realizes itself in motion, a realm that fuses dancer and onlooker, body and consciousness, thought and perception in an intensely focused presence."[2] Central to Berleant's notion of the "presentational realm" is the intersection of the respective engagement of performer and spectator in a shared moment.[3]

## THE MAGIC CIRCLE

The social space of sport is grounded in the physical space of the soccer pitch, hockey rink, basketball court, and *dohyō*, and, in its own way, in the virtual space of e-sports. The Dutch cultural historian Johan Huizinga reflected on this relationship in his pioneering study of the role of play in the formation of human cultures, *Homo Ludens* ("Man the Player"):

> All play moves and has its being with a play-ground [*sic*] marked off beforehand either materially or ideally, deliberately or as a matter of course. Just as there is no formal difference between play and ritual, so the "consecrated spot" cannot be formally distinguished from the playground. The arena, the card-table, the magic circle, the temple, the stage, the screen, the tennis court, the court of justice, etc., are all in form and function play-grounds, i.e., forbidden spots isolated, hedged round, hallowed, within which special rules obtain. All are temporary works within the ordinary world, dedicated to the performance of an act apart.[4]

This often-cited paragraph raises several topics bearing on our examination of the spatial practices of sports. Its overarching theme is Huizinga's view that there is "no formal difference" between play and ritual. Both, he argues, are practices set apart from the mundane affairs of daily life by their performance conducted according to rules of behavior applied within the material or conceptual boundaries of a playground or consecrated spot. His examples of settings range in scale from the few square feet of a card table to the thousands of square feet required for tennis courts and buildings. The items in his list are not equally tangible. Few audience members think about the material properties of a movie screen when drawn into the world projected on its surface. Even less tangible is his reference to the "magic circle." Indefinite as a physical entity, it suggests a realm of the extraordinary.

Theorists and designers of video games have found the notion of the magic circle useful as a characterization of the immersion of players in virtual environments.[5] I'm similarly drawn to its experiential implications. The term evokes the casting of a spell. I think of pregame rituals, simple or elaborate, as incantations that activate the social space of the game with the promise of an extraordinary experience for those within its embrace. The spell can be rudely shattered, however, by a spectator running onto the field, a player violating the spirit of fair play with a flagrant foul, or the horror of a serious injury. "The least deviation," Huizinga notes, "'spoils the game,' robs it of its character and makes it worthless." Unbroken, the spell allows play to bring "into an imperfect world and into the confusion of life . . . a temporary, a limited perfection," demanding "order absolute and supreme."[6] The opportunity to achieve or witness perfection is one of the great attractions of sports for athletes and spectators. In figure skating, this quest is inscribed on the ice.

Now commonly thought of in terms of spins, jumps, and lyrical turns around the rink, figure skating's original emphasis, and the source of its name (acquired in the mid-nineteenth century) was on tracing patterns—figures—that could range from simple loops to a skater's signature on the surface of the ice.[7] To this end, a game called combined skating was popular in the nineteenth and early twentieth centuries (figure 3.2). It typically involved four skaters who would transform a patch of smooth ice into a frame for play by defining a center point (oranges—highly visible and yielding if hit—were popular markers) around which they would position themselves in

A COMBINED-FIGURE ON WIMBLEDON LAKE, JANUARY, 1891. [*Frontispiece.*

Figure 3.2. Combined figure skating. Montagu S. Monier-Williams, Winter Randell Pidgeon, and Arthur Dryden, *Figure Skating Simple and Combined* (London, 1892).

opposing pairs on the circumference of a circle.[8] A member of the group designated as the caller would specify a figure, much like a square dance caller, and the partners, one pair at a time, would skate toward and past each other, incising the figure's symmetrical shape on the ice as cleanly as possible. As in a square dance, the game required the skaters to maintain awareness of their partners' actions as well as their own. Success was measured according to the precision of the realized figure and the style of execution. The game translated well from a source of bragging rights among friends to a competitive sport.

In the early years of competitive figure skating around the turn of the twentieth century, contestants (singles or pairs) would present the officials with a drawing of a pattern of their own design and be judged on the accuracy of its execution. Skating associations eventually made it easier to compare performances by assigning the shapes to be traced from standardized sets of circular "school" figures (also known as compulsory figures) that aspiring competitors were expected to master. This event was a component of international figure skating competitions until 1990, when it was eliminated to emphasize free skating, which is more expressive, audience-friendly, and telegenic.[9]

US Figure Skating followed suit after the 1999 national championship competition, but some skating organizations continue to hold compulsory figures events for skaters who enjoy their special challenges.

Standing on a smooth, unmarked area of ice amid the confusion of other skaters warming up, coaches providing final instructions, officials, and spectators, the competitor in a compulsory figures event invokes the extraordinary order of a magic circle with a gesture indicating the long axis of the assigned figure. Then, engaged in Huizinga's temporary, limited perfection and guided without the aid of external reference points by mental image and muscle memory, the skater imposes form on the blank ice, tracing and retracing the pattern on each foot. Obscured by the skater's fluid movement are the countless, fine-grain muscular adjustments made in response to centrifugal force and the friction of the metal skate edges carving the ice. Judgment of the result, in addition to assessment of the accuracy of the completed figure, evaluates the skater's carriage, pace, and smoothness. The traced figure is a transcription of the skater's presence that transforms an anonymous patch of ice into a place charged by human intent, at least until its erasure by the Zamboni ice-grooming machine for the next competitor.

The skater's performance in a compulsory figures competition is a matter of mental and physical discipline applied to the faultless realization of geometric forms on the surface of the ice. In one-on-one combat sports, such as sumo and fencing, and team sports that involve the invasion of an opponent's territory, such as soccer and basketball, competitors seek to disrupt their opponents' pursuit of perfection. The task requires creative strategic planning and tactical skill to outwit the opposition and dictate control of space and time. In chapter 1, I described golf course architects as puzzle-makers who shape the landscape to provide players with an intriguing variety of challenges in a round of eighteen holes. The malleable elements of combat and invasion sports are human bodies. As the Dutch soccer player Barry Hulshoff observed, "It is a kind of architecture on the field. It is about movement but still it is about space, about organizing space."[10] Although the physical properties of playing fields are givens, the full range of the opportunities they offer for tactical innovation may not be obvious due to the ingrained habits of conventional practices—"We've always done it this way!"—and limitations of athletic ability. The histories of the team sports of soccer, American football, and basketball illustrate how coaches and players learn to take advantage of the tactical advantage of the frame of the playing field and reimagine the game's spatial character.

## CONTROLLING THE FIELD IN SOCCER AND AMERICAN FOOTBALL

The fundamental objectives of soccer and football and the dimensions of their playing fields have been constants for more than a century, but the ways the games are played have changed dramatically. In both sports, the tactics for asserting control of the field have evolved from a narrow focus on the area occupied by the ball handler to a more expansive view that seizes competitive advantage wherever it can be found. Through the tactical positioning of players, teams seek to control spatial perception by making the field appear large and open to possibilities when on offense and small and hemmed in for the opposing defenders.

From the 1860s to the 1880s, many English soccer teams emphasized dribbling the ball straight to the goal or chasing after long kicks with a front line of six or more players whose progress would be contested by the opposing team's front line (figure 3.3). Passing, while legal, was viewed unfavorably.[11] In a match played by England and Scotland in 1877, a member of the England team, Alfred Lyttelton, challenged by a teammate on his failure to pass the ball, reportedly replied, "I am playing purely for my own pleasure, Sir!"[12] The focus on the individual ball handler assigned little strategic value to the remainder of the pitch apart from protecting the goal from deep kicks downfield.

There were competing points of view. Teams in Scotland

Figure 3.3. "Football at the Oval—England v. Scotland" (Kensington Oval, London). *The Illustrated London News*, April 12, 1879. British Library/Alamy.

were known for their "combination play" that advanced the ball with short passes as well as dribbling. Passing allowed team members to use more of the pitch by spreading out and moving the ball from side to side to outflank defenders. An early glimpse of the future of the passing game was seen in 1872 at the first international soccer match, when Scotland, despite fielding smaller players, held favored England to a draw by passing the ball around their opponents instead of trying to run through them.[13]

As the advantages of the passing game became evident, the massed front lines were replaced by alignments that spaced players in depth to provide more options for utilizing the full extent of the pitch. The 1925 revision of the offside rule, which made it easier to initiate attacks deep in an opponent's territory, inspired further refinements that facilitated transitions between offense and defense.[14] In his history of soccer tactics, *Inverting the Pyramid*, Jonathan Wilson traces the emergence of new centers of tactical innovation as the sport spread beyond Great Britain to Continental Europe and Latin America. In

Switzerland, the Austrian player-manager Karl Rappan pioneered the use of zone defense in the 1930s by assigning a player, later known as the *librero*, or sweeper, to patrol the area in front of the goalkeeper and intercept through-balls or attackers who slip past the midfield defenders. In Brazil, Zezé Moreira was among coaches in the early 1950s experimenting with expanded forms of zonal positioning throughout the pitch as an alternative to matching players one to one.[15] His tactics also encouraged players to shift from their nominal positions to reinforce teammates or to capitalize on a defensive lapse by the opponents and instigate a counterattack.

The tactical fluidity of approaches like Moreira's led some creative coaches of the mid-twentieth century to regard the pitch elastically, subject to manipulation of players' spatial perception of opportunity and risk. Of the parallel innovations to this effect in the late 1960s and early 1970s by Valeriy Lobanovskyi in Ukraine and Rinus Michels in the Netherlands, Wilson observes, "The game as they saw it was about space and how you controlled it: make the pitch big when you have the ball and it is easy to retain it; make it small when you do not and it becomes far more difficult for the opposition to keep it."[16] Thus, players in possession of the ball expand the pitch by positioning themselves, often in loose triangular groupings, so as to provide multiple options for quickly moving the ball up, down, and across the pitch to draw their opponents out of position and open an advantageous point of attack. On defense, the object is to shrink the field by converging on the ball handler, choking off passing lanes, and preventing the opponents' efforts to expand the field. These principles remain fundamental aspects of the game today and underlie strategies including the *tiki taka* possession play of long chains of short passes back and forth across the field exemplified by Barcelona under the leadership of Pep Guardiola from 2008 to 2012 as well as the high-pressure *Gegenpressing* of quickly dispossessing the opponent and counterattacking associated with the teams managed by Jürgen Klopp.

Like soccer, American football tactics have evolved from teams advancing the ball en masse to more wide-open play.

Football's core features—the gridiron, eleven players on a side, play proceeding incrementally to achieve a prescribed distance within a set number of downs—were codified in the 1880s. Signature plays of the era included the infamous flying wedge, in which a ball carrier was protected within a dense formation of his teammates running over hapless defenders, which was first inflicted by Harvard upon Yale in 1892 (figure 3.4). An early chronicler of the sport described the play as "the most original and beautiful ever seen upon a football field."[17] It was prohibited for safety reasons two years later, but the spirit of "smash-mouth" play endures.

Partly as a way of reducing injuries (and deaths) from mass plays like the flying wedge, the forward pass was legalized in 1906. Its widespread acceptance, however, was gradual, even after the Notre Dame quarterback "Gus" Dorais memorably demonstrated its efficacy in 1913 when he surprised Army by throwing the ball 40 yards downfield to Knute Rockne, who caught the pass in full stride and ran on to score a touchdown.

S. C. Gwynne recounts the history of the passing game's spatial transformation of football in *The Perfect Pass: American Genius and the Reinvention of Football.* He focuses his

Figure 3.4. "The Original Flying Wedge, Harvard's famous formation about to attack Yale," November 19, 1892. Parke H. Davis, *Football: The American Intercollegiate Game* (New York, 1911).

story on the coaching career of Hal Mumme, a key figure in the development of the "air raid" offense that upends smashmouth football's emphasis on running plays—"three yards and a cloud of dust," in the words of the legendary Ohio State University coach Woody Hayes—with a pass-first approach. Coaching high school and college teams in the 1980s and 1990s, Mumme built on the work of other inventive coaches to devise an approach that could be easily taught, open the field for the offense, and confuse defenders.

"Mesh" is a play fulfilling these objectives that Mumme adopted from the coach LaVell Edwards at Brigham Young University and perfected with assistant coach Mike Leach at Iowa Wesleyan College from 1989 to 1991 (figure 3.5). Its underlying concepts remain in use at the high school, college, and professional levels. As an offensive formation, Mesh features two pass receivers spread far to the left and right of the tackles, guards, center, and tight end at the heart of the line of scrimmage. The quarterback stands several yards behind the center, flanked by two running backs with good pass-receiving skills. When the ball is snapped, the players on offense simultaneously execute

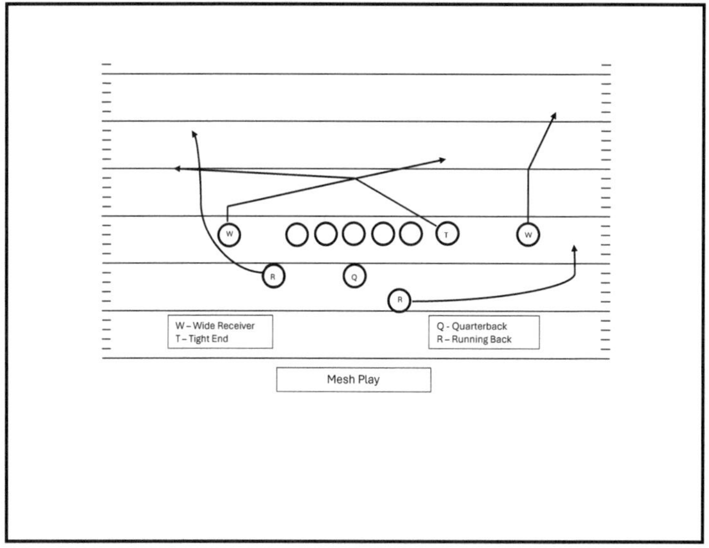


Figure 3.5. Mesh play. Diagram by author.

a burst of movements intended to confuse their opponents' assessment of the imminent threat. The wide receiver on the left wing runs a shallow route to the right, slightly downfield of and parallel to the line of scrimmage. The tight end, starting from a position near the right tackle, does the same in the opposite direction to the left, and the two players nearly touch as their routes cross, creating a traffic problem for the defenders responsible for covering them (stay with the player or protect the zone?). Meanwhile, the wide receiver on the right runs downfield toward the corner of the end zone as the two backs work with the offensive line to protect the quarterback from pass rushers before breaking off to the left and right on shallow routes downfield. If all goes according to plan, the play offers the quarterback five potential passing targets spread across and down the field. The field for the offense has become large.

Mumme devised plays such as Mesh as components of an offensive strategy intended to create opportunities by upsetting the defenders' expectations and disrupting their perception of the pace of the game. On fourth down, for instance, rather than routinely having his players turn the ball over to the opponents with a punt, he used the opportunity to press forward. As a result, Gwynne explains, "[Mumme's] players and the opposing players would see and experience different games on the field."[18] Instead of predictively shifting modes after three downs, defenders would face uncertainty and unrelenting pressure that could make the game seem very long. From the point of view of Mumme's quarterback, however, the situation would be much clearer. The receivers' planned routes present a variety of options to be assessed according to a well-rehearsed decision tree. The offense controls the tempo of play. The defenders can only react. But, like soccer players skilled at quickly responding to changes of possession, defenders devise ways to turn the tables by disrupting the timing critical to the success of plays such as Mesh. Defensive backs can jam receivers at the line of scrimmage (bump and run coverage), and speedy, agile pass rushers can slip past blockers and pressure the quarterback with the threat of a sack. The field of play is no less a laboratory for the defense as it is for the offense.

## HITTING THE TREY: SPATIAL INVENTION IN BASKETBALL

Basketball courts are crowded places. Much of the action is concentrated in the 2,350 square feet of the half court, and the ten players, five on each team, vie to create gaps through which they can dribble, pass, or shoot. Coaches have developed strategies for player positioning intended to make the court big on offense and small on defense. As in soccer, some tactics on offense are structured by flowing patterns of triangles that provide ball handlers with multiple options for passing.[19] The concept requires players to have a high degree of situational awareness and to be able to continually adjust their positions as necessary to spread the defense and create opportunities for their teammates. It can be difficult for casual spectators to recognize these tactics given the tight spacing and the speed of play. More readily apparent are the spatial implications of the three-point line (figure 3.6).

"With the exception of the forward pass in football," the cartographer and basketball analyst Kirk Goldsberry asserts, "no

Figure 3.6. Jake Barnett shoots from the corner with teammates spread along the three-point line. St. Louis University vs. Indiana State University, Chaifetz Arena, St. Louis, December 18, 2013. McClatchy-Tribune/Alamy.

rule change in American sports history has reshaped the aesthetic of its sport more than the three-point line has deformed the NBA."[20] I discussed the origins of the three-point line, implemented by the NBA in the 1979–1980 season, in chapter 1. In his book, *Sprawlball: A Visual Tour of the New Era of the NBA*, Goldsberry describes the strategic and tactical responses of players and coaches as they came to realize that the reward for shooting "from downtown," in the parlance of sportscasters, outweighs its difficulty. To capitalize on this opportunity, teams have adjusted their positioning on the court and demanded different skills from the players.[21]

The degree to which the three-point rule has changed the game in the NBA is evident in a comparison of the shooting patterns of two outstanding teams at different stages of its evolution, the 1990–1991 champion Chicago Bulls and the 2016–2017 champion Golden State Warriors. Led by Michael Jordan's aggressive inside play, the Bulls attempted only 424 three-point shots during the season, converting 155 of them for a success rate of 36 percent. Twenty-six years later, the Warriors, led by outside-shooting ace Stephen Curry, recorded 2,562 three-point attempts, sinking 982 (38 percent) of those shots.[22] The increase of three-point shots came at the expense of mid-range shooting, because the total number of shots the Warriors attempted over the season (7,140) was nearly the same as the Bulls' total (7,125). Rather than automatically taking a two-point jump shot in crowded territory outside the key, the Warriors passed to players dispersed along the three-point line. Defenders hoping to discourage the long ball had no choice but to follow it outside. The Warriors could either shoot from the perimeter or take advantage of the vacated space inside by executing quick attacks leading to a high-percentage shot near the basket or the chance of a defensive foul with the reward of a free throw. These options allow offenses to expand the contested area and utilize more of the court.

Such advantages seem obvious today, but initially they weren't readily apparent. In 1979, the *New York Times* described the three-point shot as a "gimmick" and reported the assessment of the Phoenix Suns' coach John MacLeod: "It may change our game at the end of quarters, but I'm not going to set up plays for guys to bomb from 23 feet. I think that's very boring basketball."[23] Indeed, in the first season under the rule, teams averaged only 2.8 attempts per game. Despite the example of pioneering sharpshooters (among them Brian Taylor of the San Diego Clippers and Danny Ainge of the Boston Celtics), the number of attempts increased slowly. The combination of player skill and innovative strategy came together throughout the 2010s, so that in the 2020s, NBA teams are averaging around thirty-four attempts per game. In the college game, Iowa's Caitlin Clark thrilled crowds during the 2023–2024 season by hitting 201 three-pointers—including many mid-court logo 3s—on her way to becoming the highest-scoring player in Division I basketball history for men or women. As with the playing fields of soccer, football, and other sports, the layout of the basketball court does not dictate a single way of play. Athletes and coaches must creatively explore the latent possibilities it offers, challenging the ingrained conventions of their training and envisioning the game in new ways.

## MIND GAMES

"If you are very good in mathematics and trigonometry you can be a good goalkeeper," the German keeper Manuel Neuer stated in an interview, adding, "Pythagoras would have been a good goalkeeper!"[24] Such analytic thinking in play may be observed in the move of a goalkeeper in soccer or hockey advancing from the net toward an attacker in order to narrow the angle of a shot, the deliberate positioning of a basketball player taking a shot just outside the three-point line, or a pass receiver in football astutely cutting just beyond the first down marker on an in-route. Yet, while the dimensions of the football field, soccer pitch, and basketball court do not change during a game, players can make them seem larger or smaller. By what process does a soccer player streaking toward the opponent's goal arrive in the right spot at the right time to receive a teammate's crossing pass? Geometry aside, how does the goalkeeper so quickly—seemingly instinctively—adjust her position in anticipation of the shot?

Spatial performance in sports involves both objective assessments and subjective engagement that can be examined from several interrelated perspectives. The empirical methods of trainers and coaches emphasize repetition with drills and simulated game conditions to develop deliberative behaviors—recognition of familiar situations—and what is commonly known as muscle memory, which allows an athlete to initiate many rehearsed movements, such as a fencer's parry and riposte in response to an opponent's attack, without stopping to think about them. Physiologists and neuroscientists seek to understand how our bodies accomplish this. Psychologists address states of mind and behavior. Philosophers posit interpretive frameworks. Although there is much to say from each perspective, I will touch only briefly on a few findings of neuroscience and psychology that bear on spatial practices before focusing on philosophical interpretations that shed light on the subjective experience of players and spectators drawn into a magic circle.

In *The Performance Cortex: How Neuroscience Is Redefining Athletic Genius*, the sportswriter Zach Schonbrun describes research by cognitive neuroscientists on proprioception—the perception of the position and movement of one's own body in three-dimensional space. This includes spatial orientation with respect to up/down and front/back navigation—essential processes for a gymnast executing a triple-twist dismount from the balance beam. Working at the cellular level to reveal what underlies these actions, neuroscientists trace the complex interactions of neural networks that engage multiple areas of the brain, including those associated with learning, memory, and prediction as well as those devoted to motor functions.[25] Proprioception, asserts the researcher Jia Han, "is not merely a physiological property, but rather, it has both physiological (hardware) and psychological (software) aspects."[26] Integrating sensory data of external conditions with knowledge previously acquired through training and experience, neural networks produce what might be thought of as mental mapping that allows highly skilled athletes to act as if they have eyes in the back of their heads.[27] Or, in the words of soccer player Javier "Chicharito" Hernández, Mexico's all-time leading scorer, "I don't see the goal, but I *sense* it."[28]

Colloquially, we might describe Chicharito's heightened awareness as "being in the zone," a spatial metaphor for the psychological concept of flow. As articulated by the psychologist Mihaly Csikszentmihalyi, who coined the term, a flow state occurs when one is focused on a particular activity in such a way as to discount distractions and optimally manage objectives and information.[29] With respect to athletic performance, this includes the application of strategic and tactical objectives to situational factors such as the distance and angle of approach to the goal, irregularities in the surface of the field, and the locations of other players. Athletes and others in a flow state may experience their tasks with an altered sense of time and a feeling of detachment from other concerns. This state of mind is expressed vividly in the interviews Onaje X. O. Woodbine conducted for his ethnographic study of street basketball in Boston, *Black Gods of the Asphalt: Religion, Hip-Hop, and Street Basketball* (2016). "It's just like you forget what's going on, pretty much, everything else on the outside world," a player named Tyshawn shared. "For that however much time that you're on the court, I mean that's the only thing that you're focusing on. You don't know the time of day, everything else is pretty much you're just blacked-out between those four lines. That rectangle is your whole new space for that certain time being."[30]

Alongside its psychological, physiological, and neurological aspects, Tyshawn's performance may be examined through the interpretive lens of phenomenology, a branch of philosophy addressing the way individuals experience the things—phenomena—they encounter. It includes sensations—to which proprioception may be added alongside the more familiar sight, touch, hearing, smell, and taste—and the meanings we make of them. A phenomenological approach regards our engagement with our surroundings holistically rather than through discrete subject-object relationships that isolate mind from body and self-awareness from environment. Not surprisingly, it is among the methods of inquiry employed by philosophers of sport.[31]

It also has informed architectural theory, as we've seen in the writings of Bachelard cited in chapter 1, and Pallasmaa, introduced in chapter 2.

The phenomenologist Maurice Merleau-Ponty illustrates an embodied view of spatial experience with an example of a soccer player in his book *The Structure of Behavior*:

> For the player in action the soccer field is not an "object." . . . It is pervaded with lines of force (the "yardlines" [*sic*] those which demarcate the "penalty area") and is articulated into sectors (for example, the "openings" between the adversaries) which call for a certain mode of action and which initiate and guide the action as if the player were unaware of it. The field itself is not given to him, but present as the immanent term of his practical intentions; the player becomes one with it and feels the direction of the "goal" for example, just as immediately as the vertical and the horizontal planes of his own body. It would not be sufficient to say that consciousness inhabits this milieu. At this moment consciousness is nothing other than the dialectic of milieu and action. Each maneuver undertaken by the player modifies the character of the field and establishes new lines of force in which the action in turn unfolds and is accomplished, again altering the phenomenal field.[32]

This description recalls both Chicharito "sensing" rather than "seeing" the goal and Tyshawn's perception of the rectangle of the court as his "whole new space" for the duration of play. The imaginary soccer player similarly embodies their surroundings in a way that erases distinctions between subject (the self) and object (the game's frame) and conscious thought and physical action.

Merleau-Ponty's example addresses only the perspective of a single actor. A soccer match, however, involves twenty-two players seeking to shape the phenomenal field to their own advantage. This dynamic is readily apparent in the execution of feints. A critical skill in many sports, feints include a fencer's steps back and forth to draw the opponent into an unbalanced position, a hockey player deking a defender with forehand to backhand stick work, and a soccer player's crossover step. The mechanics of a feint are learned through practice and internalized in muscle memory, but execution requires the seduction of an opponent. The philosopher of sport Kenneth Aggerholm and his colleagues describe this as a three-step process that can be understood in phenomenological terms as a holistic interaction in space and time.[33] The first step is for the player executing the feint to be noticed by the opponent. It involves the player's self-awareness in setting up the feint, the opponent's recognition of the action, and the player's awareness of the opponent's response. After attracting the opponent's attention comes the seduction, which Aggerholm describes as a spiritual duel to shape the perceptual field and pull the opponent physically and mentally off balance. At this juncture, the player executes the third step: a move that capitalizes on the advantage. A passage in *Black Gods of the Asphalt* relating Woodbine's own experience in a streetball game illustrates this process.

> [The guard] stood in front of me. He moved his chest close to mine as I dribbled the ball in my right hand. . . . I crouched low to the ground and fed the ball between my legs from right to left. I could feel him trying to read my body language. He inched closer, crowding my legs with his torso. I found a crevice in our warm embrace and gently fed the ball between my legs from left to right. . . . He inched closer, but I suddenly felt fear and panic run through his body. He had overcommitted. He was now at the mercy of my handle as I weaved the ball through the small openings between us in rhythmic fashion. . . . In desperation, he viciously hacked down on my forearms to force the referee to stop the game.[34]

In this account, Woodbine's skillful, rhythmic dribbling initiated the feint by attracting the attention of the defender and then seduced him into drawing closer in expectation of stealing the ball until, too late, he realized that he was neither in control of the tempo nor in position to react to a breakaway move. Rather than allow Woodbine to capitalize on his advantage, he interrupted the flow of play, shattering the perfection of Huizinga's magic circle, by committing a foul. The measured distances of this interaction were small but significant with respect to both players' perceptions of risk and opportunity. Woodbine's precise dribbling shielded the ball with his body and minimized exposure to a steal while increasing the defender's risk of an inadvertent foul while reaching in. The defender gave up when he realized he had taken a step too far and lost his opportunity to control the game. Space from a phenomenological perspective is embodied, relational, and subjective rather than external, measured, and objective.

## AESTHETIC ENGAGEMENT IN SPORTS

The intense engagement with the game expressed by the streetball players in Woodbine's study may be described as aesthetic. Aesthetics may not be the first thing that comes to mind when reading his description of the defender's challenge, watching a rugby scrum, or agonizing as a favorite team succumbs to a blowout. The popular sense of the term typically refers to the appreciation of beauty in the arts or an elegant athletic move and often opposes it to utility. In architecture, this view can relegate the aesthetic to something to be addressed after functional issues have been resolved, if the budget allows. Applied to sports, it can regard the aesthetic as incidental to the gritty effort of athletic excellence. What matters is the win. "It wasn't pretty," an athlete may say to a sideline reporter, "but it got the job done." The aesthetic need not be understood in binary terms. In architecture, beauty and utility can be inseparable in the case of a building or detail that elegantly fulfills its purpose. In some sports, such as ice dancing, synchronized swimming, and snowboard halfpipe, getting the job done requires mastery of explicitly aesthetic components.[35] More broadly, the strain, sweat, and even violence of athletic performance may be aesthetic.[36] A branch of philosophy known as everyday aesthetics provides a framework for integrating the objective and subjective dimensions of spatial practices.[37]

John Dewey was a forerunner of this approach (aspects of his philosophy of pragmatism also anticipate and complement phenomenology).[38] In *Art as Experience* he defines experience as "the result, the sign, and the reward" of the attentive interaction of a person (he uses the more abstract term "organism") with their surroundings.[39] He observes that possessing "a unity that gives it its name, *that* meal, that storm, that rupture of friendship" distinguishes aesthetic experience from less engaged levels of interaction. He adds that this unity "is constituted by a single *quality* that pervades the entire experience in spite of the variation of its constituent parts."[40] For Dewey, the aesthetic refers to the perception, development, appreciation, and enjoyment of the distinctive quality constituting an experience. It is a state of heightened engagement with the implication of action rather than of detached reflection.

The concept invites consideration across a variety of cultural activities, including the arts and sports, that often are regarded in isolation. In sports, reflections of Dewey's notion of aesthetic experience are evident in the almost uncanny ability of athletes to recall in exacting detail the circumstances of a particular pitch thrown or goal scored decades after the fact. These actions had been performed in a state of concentration that internalized them in memory as *that* pitch and *that* goal. Dewey's emphasis on the degree of engagement with a particular quality reconciles the split between aesthetics and utility. Strikeouts and goals scored fulfill the competitive objectives of a sport, but they can be performed and witnessed in a state of heightened engagement that makes them aesthetic.

The philosopher of sport and basketball coach Tim Elcombe draws on Dewey's view of human experience as embodied, structured, and continuous to make a cheerfully provocative case for basketball as the "world's most 'phenomenal' game."[41] Attributes of the sport that heighten engagement are the correspondence of the dimensions of the court and the number of players that affords continuous opportunities for the involvement of all players; the opposing, elevated baskets that establish horizontal and vertical elements to the game; and the interplay of the time ticking away on the game clock and the players' ability to stop it at strategic points with time-outs. More than any other sport, he asserts, basketball "reveals to us the potential to play *with* and *in* time and space."[42]

Swimmers don't get to stop and start time—the pace of a race is relentless—but they engage with the setting of their sport in extraordinary ways (figure 3.7). In the water, buoyancy offsets gravity, but the viscosity of the aquatic environment also imposes resistance, affects sight and hearing, and conducts the kinetic energy of waves generated by competitors that move across the pool and reflect off the walls and floor. Through countless yet mindful repetitions, swimmers train their proprioception to optimize the orientation of their bodies to minimize drag and to maximize the power of their strokes.[43] When all goes smoothly, swimmers can feel they are flying, no longer earthbound.

This aesthetic response, in the words of philosopher Arnold Berleant discussing architecture and landscape architecture among other arts in his book *Art and Engagement*, emerges from "a sense of environment as a field of forces continuous with

Figure 3.7. Swimmers in an Olympic-size pool. H. Mark Weidman Photography/Alamy.

the organism [the swimmer in this instance], a condition where organism acts on surroundings and surroundings on organism and where, in fact, no real demarcation divides them."[44] "What makes this field experience aesthetic," he argues, "is the central place of its perceptual qualities."[45] These qualities involve more than processing sensory inputs. They constitute a comprehensive notion of awareness involving memory and imagination. For Berleant, the environmental arts of architecture and landscape architecture, products of which include the playing fields of sports, "create the human realm, the possibilities of vision, audition, and movement, the scope of actual perception."[46]

In this spirit, "the task of architecture," the architect Pallasmaa asserts, "is not to beautify or 'humanise' the world of everyday fact, but to open a view into the second dimension of our consciousness, the reality of dreams, images and memories."[47] For the philosopher Michael Novak, sports arenas and stadiums can open such views. "Even a new stadium . . . is a place where tradition instantaneously begins. Impoverished in memory, a new arena is a tabula rasa for new impressions. Records are set. Achievements are fixed in memory."[48] Turning to the athlete on the playing field, he states: "When an athlete kicks at the dust of the infield, or digs his cleats into turf or carpet, or squeaks his sneakers on the reflection-yielding floorboards, he gains a sense of concentration: all the hours of practice, all the years of discipline, all the frustrations of getting ready, have their focus here. The arena draws inward the multiplicities of life and weaves them into a tapestry. Once woven, the threads remain entwined forever."[49]

## AESTHETIC ENGAGEMENT AND THE SPECTATOR

Beyond observing a sport or having a vested interest in its outcome, spectators project their own bodily awareness on the playing field. Prior experience playing a sport may enhance this engagement, but it is not essential. We can appreciate athletic performance as an extension of everyday movements. A memory of walking on a log spanning a stream, for instance, provides a personal, physical reference to the actions of a gymnast on the balance beam.

In his examination of the aesthetic experience of spectatorship, the literary critic and philosopher Hans Gumbrecht writes of the dual appeal for spectators and athletes alike of *agon*, the ancient Greek term encompassing competitive struggle, and the related notion of *arête*, the ideal of excellence. The attraction can inspire an aesthetic experience of athletic beauty, which he considers on a spectrum with dispassionate analysis at one pole and emotionally invested communion, the realm of partisan fans, at the other.[50] Gumbrecht's terms recall the primal aesthetic impulses, Apollonian and Dionysian, postulated by Friedrich Nietzsche in *The Birth of Tragedy*.[51] Reason and order govern the Apollonian impulse; unrestrained emotion fuels the Dionysian. Both can be found on the playing field.

The writer Roger Angell eloquently evokes the analytic, Apollonian mode of spectatorship in spatial terms in the chapter devoted to "the interior stadium" in his collection of essays on baseball, *The Summer Game*.

> Sit quietly in the upper stand and look at the field. Half close your eyes against the sun, so that the players recede a little, and watch the movements of baseball. The pitcher, immobile on the mound, holds the inert white ball, his little lump of physics. Now, with abrupt gestures, he gives it enormous speed and direction, converting it suddenly into a line, a moving line. The batter, wielding a plane, attempts to intercept the line and acutely alter it, but he fails; the ball, a line again, is redrawn to the pitcher, in the center of this square, the diamond. . . . From our perch, we can sometimes see three or four or more such geometries appearing at the same instant on the green board below us, and, mathematicians that we are, can sense their solution even before they are fully drawn. It is neat, it is pretty, it is satisfying. Scientists speak of the profoundly moving

> aesthetic beauty of mathematics, and perhaps the baseball field is one of the few places where the rest of us can glimpse this mystery.[52]

Sometimes, a glimpse is all a spectator gets. There was little in the way of geometric order in the bottom of the eighth inning of the wildcard playoff game between the Atlanta Braves and the St. Louis Cardinals in 2012.[53] With one out, runners on first and second base, and his team trailing 6–3, Atlanta's Andrelton Simmons hit a fly ball into shallow left field. The St. Louis shortstop and left fielder both charged to make the catch, but the ball fell untouched between them. The flub would have allowed Simmons and the runners to load the bases had not an umpire's upraised arm signaled an infraction of the infield fly rule, a regulation intended to prevent ball-handling shenanigans by infielders. In his judgment, the St. Louis shortstop, technically an infielder even when standing in the outfield, was in a position to catch the ball with ordinary effort and should have completed the play. The batter was out, the base runners returned to their initial positions, and the Atlanta fans, failing to see why the rule applied to a play in the outfield, went berserk. They demonstrated their outrage with a fusillade of debris that halted the game for nineteen minutes. That day, Turner Field belonged to Dionysius rather than Apollo, the magic circle's ideal of perfection shattered and recast by the fans' collective sense of the injustice of the official's potentially game-changing decision (St. Louis held its lead and won the game).

Video review at the time was not permitted for such circumstances, so any further thoughts the official may have had about the shortstop's positioning, or the difficulty of the play, were dependent on his memory of what he saw as the play unfolded. Video replay was, however, available to the fans in the stands (not to mention everyone on the field) watching the stadium video screen and the multitude of television viewers at home and in sports bars. All saw the play looped over and over with a variety of camera angles offering multiple perspectives and points of departure for debating the call. For everyone other than the officials, the spatial and temporal experience of the game was not only a matter of being in a moment but of having that instance of real time mediated and transformed with respect to point of view and duration by video replays.

## THE GIFT OF GRACE

Alongside extremes of dispassionate analysis and frenzy, aesthetic experience of spectatorship can involve collective empathy for athletes playing with abandon beyond all expectations. Some of these performances become iconic events celebrated for decades after their occurrence. Among these is the winning "Goal of the Century" that the great Argentinian soccer player Diego Maradona scored in the 1986 World Cup quarterfinal match between Argentina and England. After receiving a pass from a teammate in his own half of the pitch, Maradona headed downfield on what became a ten-second, sixty-yard run during which he wound his way past four of England's players, stepped by the goalkeeper with a feint, and deposited the ball in the net. For many of the more than 114,000 spectators who witnessed the play in Mexico City's Estadio Azteca and the global television audience, not to mention viewers subsequently entranced by video recordings, Maradona embodied a free-spirited force that simultaneously tethered the ball to his feet and repelled his highly skilled opponents. Transcending technical achievement, his play inspired feelings of wonder and grace.

Grace has been a contentious term for philosophers writing about the aesthetics of sports.[54] Some define it in terms of economy of movement. Gumbrecht describes it as a quality seemingly separate from consciousness and offers as an example the hypnotic effect of the rhythmic strides of speed skaters turning lap after lap in a long-distance race.[55] Taking a similar position, Christopher Cordner emphasizes "the *appearance* of effortlessness" and writes, "It is as if the originating energy of the movement flows through the graceful mover from somewhere beyond her, rather than coming from her own effort."[56] He allows, "Grace can strike us as *wonderful*, and that sense of it seems to be categorically different from its being a pleasing appearance, even an extremely pleasing one."[57] To this, I would add the term's metaphysical or spiritual connotation as a transmutation of the concrete to the intangible that exceeds our immediate understanding. "In beholding the spectacle of grace," the philosopher David Michael Levin observes, "our productive imagination surpasses its sensible ground, and we witness the joining of earth and Sky."[58] His statement addresses ballet rather than sports. Discussing the mid-twentieth century masterworks by George Balanchine, Levin explains how he finds grace in details of the choreography as well as in moments of dramatic intensity. The exacting craft of choreographer and dancer manipulates space and time in such a way that the mechanics appear incidental. What matters is wonder.

Manifestations of grace in a dance performance arise in the service of aesthetic intent. This also is the case for sports involving artistic criteria. Performances in figure skating, half-pipe snowboarding, and artistic gymnastics, for instance, are based on carefully planned, smoothly executed movements. Some athletes transcend the demonstration of pleasing technical facility. The gymnast Simone Biles evokes flight more than earth-bound jumps in her soaring vaults, flips, and dismounts.

Grace also arises in sports judged without artistic criteria. Woodbine describes a streetball game in which the spectators were drawn together for a freeze-frame instant by the magnitude and focus of a player's leaping move at the net. He faltered and time moved on, yet for the witnesses, as Woodbine recalls, "it was the greatest play of the tournament, and he had not even touched the rim."[59] The failure to score was of less consequence than the gift of grace: indeterminate, fleeting in duration, but enduring in memory.

Grace can be experienced by athletes as well as spectators. Skateboarding offers an example. Borden describes skateboarders' mastery of forces to artfully execute the ollie, that seemingly gravity-defying trick of the rider soaring into the air with the board as an extension of the body. First perfected by the American skateboarder Alan Gelfand in 1978, it has become a fundamental skill practiced assiduously by young riders around the world. When performed smoothly with each action made in perfect time, the execution of the rear-foot pop, jump, and front-foot slide to clear an obstacle or simply for the pleasure of hovering above the pavement achieves a "delicate relation," in Borden's words, "between body, board, terrain and gravitational force."[60] In these moments, the rider may feel herself joining earth and sky. "Making your board an extension of your body is control of your soul," writes a contributor to the skateboarding magazine *Thrasher* quoted by Borden.[61]

## EXPLORATION AND REDEFINITION

The wheels, trucks, and deck of the skateboard are extensions of the rider's feet that register the texture of the pavement—smooth asphalt, say, or pebbled concrete—and stimulate memory, creativity, and physiological mechanisms of muscular response. It is a study of architectural elements that often escape notice. "This process," Borden writes, "takes place through a very precise (although undoubtably limited) *questioning* of architecture put forward by skateboarding. What is this architectural form for? To what purpose can it be put? What is the relation of ground, verticals, textures, surfaces?"[62]

Athletes in other sports ask similar questions in their efforts to master the settings in which they perform. Surfers read the swell of approaching waves to determine the direction of the break and the optimal position to catch a ride. Golfers lining up their putts assess the subtle slopes of the green, the texture of the grass, and the force of the wind. Skateboarders, parkour practitioners, and freerunners are known for pursuing their inquiries to a degree that overturns prevailing assumptions about purpose and use.[63]

Although these sports may be performed in dedicated settings, many practitioners seek out features in everyday environments to challenge their skills. "Parkour eyes" ("skateboard eyes" for boarders) describes the ability to envision ordinary landscapes as laboratories for spatial exploration. Practitioners find new meanings by exploring the dimensions, textures, and structural behavior of stair railings and benches with their vaults and slides. In so doing, observes the philosopher of sport Signe Højbjerre Larsen, they "develop a certain perception of where material objects in urban places are bound together by routines of significant movements; routines of movements that are invisible to the non-skilled but are perceptible to the cultivated eyes of the practitioners."[64] A parkour practitioner seeking a challenging site for a vault views a park bench in very different ways than a pedestrian looking for a place to sit. The potential conflict is a reminder that while sporting events are extraordinary, their spatial practices operate within broader social contexts of behavior and identity, the topic to which I turn next.

CHAPTER 4

# SPORTS, SPACE, AND CULTURE

In the twenty-third minute of the soccer match between the Netherlands and Sweden in the group play stage of the 1974 FIFA World Cup, Johan Cruyff, the Netherlands' captain, received a pass deep in Sweden's territory. Defender Jan Olsson quickly closed off opportunities for a crossing pass or a shot on goal. Apparently stymied, Cruyff turned as if to retreat but abruptly pivoted over the ball and reversed direction. Olsson followed the feint and inadvertently opened a gap through which Cruyff played the ball to his teammates converging on the goal. Although it did not lead to a score, the innovative stepover move, now a staple of soccer training, achieved victory at the tactical heart of soccer, the contest to create and control space.

Cruyff was the visionary leader of Ajax Amsterdam and the Dutch national teams of the 1970s (he also is revered as a player for FC Barcelona and as manager of Barcelona and Ajax). With manager Rinus Michels he practiced a mode of play known as Total Football that blended individual creativity and teamwork. Visualizing the pitch elastically, players did not maintain prescribed positions but continually adjusted their roles according to tactical circumstances. Total Football, for David Winner, the author of *Brilliant Orange: The Neurotic Genius of Dutch Soccer*, embodies a quality of Dutch culture that values both collective systemization and individual expression. In describing this spirit, Winner notes similarities between the premises of Total Football and the thought of Dutch architects including Aldo van Eyck and Herman Hertzberger. In what may be a first for a book on the sport, he cites passages of architectural theory, including this from Hertzberger's *Lessons for Students in Architecture*: "Each form must be interpretable in the sense that it must be capable of taking on different roles. And it can only take on those different roles if the different meanings are contained in the essence of the form."[1] Hertzberger's call for multivalence challenged mid-twentieth-century doctrines of functionalism that emphasized singular relationships of use and form. He applied his theory in the design of an office building for the Centraal Beheer insurance company in Apeldoorn, the Netherlands (1972). Interlocking, nonhierarchical spaces simultaneously provide well-defined workstations and facilitate interaction among the staff. The parts are individualized expressions of the whole. Similarly, Total Football challenged entrenched practices in soccer that rigidly defined players' roles.

In conversations with players and coaches, Winner was struck by the way they described the game in spatial terms. "It is all about making space and coming into space," the veteran player Barry Hulshoff observed.[2] Winner interpreted such language as an expression of a deeply rooted sensibility inspired by the openness of the country's landscape and its precarious relationship to the sea. "The Dutch think innovatively, creatively and abstractly about space in their football," he suggests, "because for centuries they have had to think innovatively about space in every other area of their lives."[3] This is not to say that the emergence of Total Football in the Netherlands was the inevitable result of exclusively Dutch attributes. Related innovations were implemented in the middle decades of the twentieth century by teams in other countries, notably England, Austria, Hungary, and Ukraine, as tactics and talent crossed borders. Whatever the sources, the principles of Total Football—make the pitch big when you have the ball; make it small when you do not—resonated within sociocultural contexts beyond the boundaries of the pitch. However much feats such as the Cruyff turn draw participants and observers into a magic circle differentiated from the routines of daily life, sports reflect, by design, tradition, or selective interpretation, values external to the game itself. In this chapter I examine ways the spatial practices of sports affirm and, on occasion, challenge collective values of identity and behavior.

## FROM LOCATION TO PLACE

The settings and performative practices of soccer and other sports are means of place making. *Place* in this sense refers to more than location, materiality, and function. Since the mid-twentieth century, scholars in the social sciences, humanities, and environmental design professions have applied the term to describe subjective individual and collective engagement with buildings and landscapes.[4] The characterization of a location as a place involves the memories and aspirations of human presence. This meaning corresponds to Novak's evocation of sports arenas as "our cathedrals" in *The Joy of Sports*.[5] The link is not the materiality of architectural grandeur, but the role of cathedrals and arenas as settings where people gather to enact familiar rituals. Like religious monuments, shrines of sports such as Lambeau Field, home of the Green Bay Packers football team in Wisconsin, or Wembley Stadium in London, home of the English national soccer team and the Football Association Final, draw pilgrims not only to attend a game but also to be present at the site. Kōshien Stadium near Kobe, Japan, built in 1924 as the setting for the national high school baseball tournaments, is the site of a moving ritual in which the losing players collect dirt from the infield to spread at their home ballparks to inspire them in seasons to come.[6] High school football stadiums and more modest venues such as playground soccer pitches, rural baseball diamonds, and backyard hockey rinks may not bedazzle the eye like a storied collegiate or professional stadium, draw throngs of tourists, or become settings for national rituals. But they, too, can hold special significance for the players and spectators who invest themselves in the games and local rituals performed within their boundaries. Photographers have taken note of such places and conveyed their hold on the imagination in collections such as Neville Gabie's portfolio of soccer goalposts around the world, Hans van der Meer's books documenting lower league soccer pitches in Europe, and Jeff Wilson's portraits of high school football fields in Texas.[7]

A playing field is a locus of possibilities and memories. Echoes of its significance may be perpetuated even after it has been taken over for other purposes. Sometimes, this is done by the retention of suggestive features. In Pittsburgh, the home plate used in the final game played at Forbes Field, home of the Pirates baseball team for sixty years prior to their moves to Three Rivers Stadium and PNC Park, is preserved under glass in the lobby floor of mammoth Posvar Hall on the campus of the University of Pittsburgh, close to its original location. Still in situ across the street is a fragment of the red brick outfield wall. Adjacent to it is a small venue for softball, Mazeroski Field, where the sounds of "hey batter, batter" and (aluminum) bats making contact with the ball can still be heard. Annually on October 13, Pirates fans gather for a ritual viewing on video monitors of the seventh game of the 1960 World Series when Bill Mazeroski hit the celebrated "shot heard 'round the world" recorded on television that I noted in chapter 2.[8]

A more allusive approach to memorializing the site of a demolished stadium is demonstrated in *The Trophy Room*, a mixed-media installation Gabie completed in 2001 in Middlesbrough, a large town in northern England (figure 4.1).[9] The project commemorates Ayresome Park, the storied home of the

Figure 4.1. View of the former site of Ayresome Park, Middlesbrough, UK, showing a feature of Neville Gabie's installation *The Trophy Room* (2001). Stephen Pond/PA Images/Alamy.

Middlesbrough professional soccer club for ninety-two years, replaced in the late 1990s by a housing development (since 1995, the Boros have played in Riverside Stadium, built in another part of town). Gabie's installation seeds evocations of game-day life throughout the new residential neighborhood. Stainless steel studs set into the pavement of driveways and streets mark the location of the touchlines and center circle, a bronze soccer ball embedded on the front stoop of a house locates one of the penalty spots, and a bronze puddle marks the soggy spot where Pak Doo-ik scored the match-winning goal in North Korea's upset of Italy in the group stage of the 1966 World Cup. These features offer prompts for retelling the history of the community that differentiates it from otherwise similar housing developments.

## REPRESENTATIONS OF NATIONAL IDENTITY

The settings and performance of sports also can be emblems of national identity. Grand Sumo, long celebrated as the national sport of Japan despite the greater popularity of baseball, comprises six tournaments held annually in Tokyo, Osaka, Nagoya, and Fukuoka. The bouts are framed by pageantry and rituals evoking Shinto religious practices, courtly ceremonies, and the moral code governing the lives of the athletes and officials. Publications by the Japan Sumo Association, the sport's governing body, link sumo to the mythological origins of the Japanese people and assert the continuity of its practice for over 1,700 years.[10] Historians of sumo, however, present a more nuanced story that shows how the sport's seemingly timeless traditions are constructions, some as recent as the twentieth century, responding to the intersecting interests of athletic competition, governmental authority, and commercial profit.[11]

Sumo became distinct from other forms of wrestling and martial arts during the Edo period (1600–1866).[12] The ruling Tokugawa shogunate regulated competitions and awarded monopolies for the right to stage them to families it favored. Bouts were held outdoors in informal settings that could accommodate a crowd, such as the courtyard of a temple, a corner or widening of a street, or a stretch of riverbank. Unruly conduct triggered by freewheeling action and blurred distinctions between competitors and spectators threatened official tolerance of the sport, and by the late seventeenth century, bouts were confined to a defined area—the *dohyō*—restricted to athletes and officials. Beyond separating wrestlers and spectators, the invention of the *dohyō* transformed how the sport was played and the body type associated with elite wrestlers. The goal of the contest changed from incapacitation to displacement by forcing one's opponent to step out of the ring or to touch the ground with any part of the body other than the feet. Dominance of the relatively small space (half the diameter of an Olympic freestyle wrestling ring) favors athletes who are large, yet agile. Besides defining boundaries, the *dohyō* provides a consistent spatial frame that can be replicated in various venues. To further differentiate the sport from informal competitions and to appeal to aristocratic taste, the governing families introduced rituals of consecration and purification re-created from scattered historic references that remain features of Grand Sumo today. The ring consecration ceremony (*dohyō matsuri*) at the start of a tournament involves referees who invite the presence and protection of Shinto deities (*kami*) with prayer and offerings. Before each bout, the wrestlers practice rituals of purification including sipping sanctified water and tossing handfuls of salt into the ring. The closing bow ritual (*yumi-tori-shiki*) is led by a wrestler who performs a series of movements with a bamboo bow to banish evil spirits.

The configuration of the *dohyō* reinforces the character of the competition as a ritualistic performance (figure 4.2).[13] Conforming to strict requirements governing materials and assembly, the *dohyō* is an earthen platform, 34 to 60 centimeters high, covered with a layer of sand. Low bales of straw partially buried in the platform outline the ring, which has a diameter of 4.55 meters (15 *shaku* in traditional Japanese units of measurement; this dimension was fixed in 1931). Two short, white lines (*shikirisen*) at the center of the ring mark the wrestlers' starting positions. The regularity of the circle is broken at the four cardinal directions by bales slightly set out from

Figure 4.2. Grand Sumo at the Fukuoka Kokusai Center, Fukuoka, Japan, 2009. Christian Kober 1/Alamy.

the circumference. They represent rainwater drains from the sport's open-air origins.

Grand Sumo moved indoors in 1909 as the principal occupant of the Kokugikan (National Skill/Sport Hall) in Tokyo, designed by Tatsuno Kingo, one of the first Japanese architects to have a Westernized architectural education. In appearance, the building would have been at home in European or American cities (figure 4.3).[14] The image might seem at odds with the carefully cultivated Japanese traditions of sumo, but in the context of the Meiji Restoration's agenda of modernization, the imposing, nearly twelve-thousand-seat, domed arena asserted sumo's equivalence to Western sports. It expressed modernity on Japanese terms.

At the heart of the steel and brick structure, the earthen *dohyō* was ritually constructed for each tournament. Recalling sumo's original outdoor settings, it was surmounted by a wooden roof supported by four columns; but unlike the earlier structures, which functioned as simple shelters, its design, based on the roof types of ancient Shinto temples, had an expressive role that reinforced appreciation of the sport's mythic origins. When the Japan Sumo Association moved the Tokyo Grand

Figure 4.3. Ryōgoku Kokugikan, Tokyo. Tatsuno Kingo, architect, opened 1909. Flasksrw/Wikimedia Commons.

Sumo tournaments to a new building, the Kuramae Kokugikan, in 1950, it retained the roof as an iconic feature of the *dohyō* but eliminated the columns—a striking alteration—to provide clear sightlines for television broadcasts. The heavy roof (*tsuri-yane*) floated above the *dohyō*, suspended from the ceiling of the arena by cables. The convention continues in the Ryōgoku Kokugikan, the venue for the sport in Tokyo since 1985 (the architect was Takashi Sugiyama), and the other sites of the Grand Sumo circuit.

Grand Sumo illustrates how the settings and performative aspects of sports can be designed to reinforce the constructions of political and cultural identity. Other examples are the revivals of hurling in Ireland and *calcio storico* in Florence. Hurling, an ancient stick-and-ball game resembling field hockey and lacrosse, gained new life in the late nineteenth century as an expression of the Gaelic Revival.[15] It takes its name from the distinctive, netless stick—the hurley (*camán*)—and is played by fifteen-member teams on rectangular fields such as the venerable Croke Park in Dublin, which may measure as much as 145 by 90 meters (considerably larger than the 100 by 70 meter maximum of a rugby pitch). *Calcio storico Fiorentina,* a ball game with the most violent qualities of rugby, soccer, and mixed martial arts, was played in Florence in the sixteenth century but had fallen out of favor by the eighteenth century. Its present incarnation dates to 1930, when the Fascist government revived it as an instrument of *italianità,* the program to forge Italian identity. To this end, *calcio storico* was promoted as an indigenous antecedent that predisposed Italians to their embrace of soccer despite the latter's British origins.[16] Scrubbed of its Fascist associations, *calcio storico* today celebrates Florentine identity more than Italian nationalism. It is played only in an annual tournament by teams representing the city's four historic districts. The venue is the historic Piazza di Santa Croce transformed for the occasion into a stadium with bleachers surrounding the rectangular playing field, which is surfaced with a thick layer of sand over the paving stones. At each end is a 1.2-meter fence over which the twenty-seven-person teams attempt to throw, kick, or otherwise project the ball despite largely unrestricted efforts of their opponents to prevent the goal.

Associations with a mythic past also pervade cricket and American baseball. "The cricket landscape," Bale writes of the game in Great Britain, "is invariably projected in writing, on canvas, on stage and on celluloid as a nostalgic, rustic idyll" with the game set in a village green framed by a parish church, modest but well-tended houses, and glimpses of the countryside beyond.[17] He explains how these features typically are rendered to evoke the game's origins in southern England even though, per capita, most cricket is played in the industrial north on urban grounds that historically have received little attention in popular depictions of the sport.[18] It's a nostalgic vision that privileges the genteel way of life celebrated in the patriotic song "There'll Always Be an England," written in 1939 by Ross Parker and Hughie Charles: "Though worlds may change and go awry / While there is still one voice to cry / There'll always be an England."

In the United States, similar associations color the reputation of baseball. Promoting the game to middle-class audiences in the second half of the nineteenth century, entrepreneurs such as Albert Spalding mythologized its origins in an American Eden, a realm of virtuous, self-sufficient, cash-paying farmers and tradespeople.[19] Cultural anthropologist Bradd Shore describes the game as spatially modeling an enduring tension in mainstream American culture between communitarian and individualistic values.[20] He notes, for example, the lopsided confrontation of a lone batter at home plate in the corner of the diamond against nine opponents spread across the field. The batter's object is to put the ball in play and run the bases in such a way as to elude the opposition, circumnavigate the diamond, and return home safely. The game emphasizes individual achievement in the duel between batter and pitcher that initiates the action but also rewards the contributions of teammates. Short of hitting a home run, the batter's progress as a baserunner depends on those who follow to keep the inning alive. The pitcher, meanwhile, relies on the collective efforts of infielders and outfielders to corral balls hit into play and to thwart the progress of baserunners—neatly illustrated by the teamwork of a perfectly executed 6–4–3 double play (shortstop to second base to first base).[21]

The term *ballpark* in the United States has cultural resonance similar to the nostalgic associations of cricket fields in Great Britain. Paul Goldberger takes up this topic in *Ballpark: Baseball in the American City*: "The very idea of baseball is itself an example of *rus in urbe* [an illusion of the countryside within the city], a way in which city folk might briefly break away from the grit and noise and pressures of the harsh city and indulge in the delight of rusticity."[22] Architecturally, ballparks present fans with layered transitions from city streets or asphalt parking lots through crowded stadium concourses to the spatial release of the first glimpse of the verdant playing field. Tantalizingly close, the perfectly manicured grass and neatly raked base paths beckon but remain off limits to all except the players and other persons granted the privilege of occupying it.

Rural ballparks have different connotations than urban stadiums. There is no opposition of city and country; rather, the playing field represents a break from the landscape of agrarian work and marks a gathering place for community life. The iconic literary representation of this ideal is the ballpark the fictional farmer Ray Kinsella carved out of an Iowa cornfield in W. P. Kinsella's novel *Shoeless Joe* and the movie version, *Field of Dreams* (the reconstructed set in Dyersville, Iowa, has become a sort of shrine and photo destination). Lovingly crafted, the field represents a promise rather than an end. "If you build it, he will come," proclaims the mysterious voice that motivates Ray's endeavor in the novel.[23] The "he" was gender specific.

## WHO GETS TO PLAY?

On opposite sides of a street on the campus of the University of Texas at Austin stand two well-appointed ballparks, UFCU Disch-Falk Field and Red and Charline McCombs Field. They are, respectively, the homes of the university's varsity baseball and softball teams. To the uninitiated, it wouldn't be unreasonable to identify both facilities as baseball stadiums, but they house separate branches on the family tree of bat-and-ball games. Although the fundamental objectives and procedures of the two sports are similar, softball is played on a smaller field with a larger ball pitched underhand, and there are differences in procedural rules and tactics. Most notably, the games played on the two fields are gendered—at the high school and collegiate level, men play baseball, women play softball—unlike the action in the adjacent tennis stadium, where all players use the same courts. The impressive facilities at UT for baseball and softball may be viewed in one respect as positive recognition of male and female athletes alike, but they also are legacies of a gender divide regarding appropriate roles for girls and women in American culture.

Baseball does not have inherent aspects that make it better suited for men than women, and in the late nineteenth and early twentieth centuries women as well as men played the game at a variety of amateur and professional levels. As the twentieth century progressed, however, baseball became codified as an exclusively male sport. Exceptions to the norm were women who played alongside men in the Negro American League and on the female teams of the All-American Girls Professional Baseball League (celebrated in the 1992 movie *A League of Their Own*) that found a niche during the war years from 1943 to 1954.[24] Little League Baseball (until 1972) and Major League Baseball and its minor league affiliates (from 1952 to 1992) instituted rules prohibiting female players. USA Baseball did not organize a national women's team until 2004, sixty years after the formation of the men's team. Softball was offered up as the alternative.

Initially known by a variety of names including indoor baseball, kitten ball, and mush ball, softball originated in Chicago in 1887 as a way to play baseball indoors during the winter months.[25] Adapting to the dimensions of gymnasiums and other appropriated interior spaces, the game employed a smaller diamond and a large, soft ball that would not travel as far as a regular baseball. These practices carried over when the game eventually was taken outdoors as a warm-weather sport. Today's NCAA and high-school softball diamonds have 60-foot baselines (the same as Little League baseball), unlike the 90-foot baselines of baseball. The recommended maximum depth of the NCAA softball outfield is 235 feet, 165 feet less than an NCAA baseball outfield. Apart from gendered high school and college teams, softball is played by people of all genders and ages in a variety of casual and competitive formats, including batter-friendly slow-pitch and the more demanding fast-pitch games.

Baseball, for the most part, remains a men's game and is a prime example of the sociologist Jean-Marie Brohm's view of sports as profitable commodities maintained to justify and reinforce an established order—social norms of masculinity in this case.[26] Historically, the gendered conventions of baseball and softball have been buttressed by claims based on unfounded assumptions such as the smaller fields of softball being less taxing on women's bodies, but they linger even as the rationalizations have been proven frivolous, overt prohibitions in baseball are falling away, and once inviolate barriers are becoming more permeable. Women's competitive softball in the meantime thrives with a proud, self-sustaining culture.[27] The game has distinctive strategies and traditions. Gifted players such as the shortstop Dot Richardson (UCLA and US Olympic Team) and the pitcher Cat Osterman (University of Texas at Austin and US Olympic Team) inspire emulation. Gendered but not always second class, softball diamonds, as at the University of Texas, have their place alongside baseball diamonds on high school and college campuses across the United States.

## THE RIGHT WAY TO PLAY

Insistence on a "right way" of play beyond adherence to procedural rules is a familiar aspect of a sport. Actions that show disrespect for opponents and the accepted spirit of the game, such as a baseball player making too much of a show after hitting a home run, can disrupt a competition and incite bench-clearing brawls. In addition to keeping the peace, the notion of the right way of play can be used to uphold certain social hierarchies, embrace participants who conform to them, and exclude others.

This was the case in the Anglo-Canadian appropriation of the Indigenous peoples' sport of lacrosse in the mid-nineteenth century (figure 4.4). Historians of lacrosse have identified a match played between members of the Kanien'kehá:ka (Mohawk) Nation from Kahnawà:ke (Caughnawaga) and Anglo-Canadians from Montréal on August 29, 1844.[28] Growing enthusiasm for the game among Anglo-Canadians led to the founding of the Montreal Lacrosse Club in 1856. Four years later, William George Beers, a nineteen-year-old player just beginning his career as a dentist in Montréal, set out rules and instructions in a pamphlet, which he subsequently expanded in a book. His objective was to transform what he regarded as the exciting but unruly game of Indigenous people into the official sport of the new nation that he and his contemporaries envisioned as modern and white.

Beers acknowledged the skill of Indigenous players but found their tactics lacking in "science." "A sensible, thoroughly civilized people cannot, and should not," he wrote, "play Lacrosse in the manner of the Indian. The fact that they may beat the

Figure 4.4. Lacrosse match, Montréal club vs. Mohawks of Kahnawà:ke, *Canadian Illustrated News*, June 18, 1870. McCord Stewart Museum, Montreal.

pale-face, is more a proof of their superior physical nature, than any evidence of their superior science. They play on their old principle of war, viz.: to have the most men at the critical points of attack and defence, and obey no arrangement of any kind."[29] The revised game, he asserted, "improved and reduced to rule by the whites, employs the greatest combination of physical activity white men can sustain in recreation, and is as much superior to the original as civilization is to barbarism."[30]

Beers's codification of lacrosse as an organized sport imbued with Anglo-Canadian values had spatial implications. His understanding of a "scientific approach" emphasized positional play and teamwork in contrast to the bunching and lack of tactical discipline that he ascribed to the Indigenous game. The dispersed alignments he favored placed greater emphasis on passing the ball from player to player through the air. To facilitate this strategy, Anglo-Canadian players fitted their sticks with larger heads than those favored by Indigenous players. Positional play and passing were particularly effective on more compact fields than the playing grounds of Indigenous peoples, some of whom set goals a half-mile or more apart. While Beers did not specify maximum or minimum dimensions in his initial set of rules, he observed that a 200-yard field was "a fair length" for competitions with twelve players on a side (modern lacrosse fields are 110 yards long). He also noted that among the distinguishing features of the Anglo-Canadian game was its "being restricted by that mark of civilization and trespass, the fence."[31] These views anticipated the standardization of boundaries in lacrosse and correspond to the emergence of quantitative approaches to defining the physical frames of sports elsewhere in the Anglo world. In 1863, for instance, the Football Association in Great Britain issued its first rule book, which required soccer pitches to have corner flags and conform to a maximum length (200 yards) and minimum width (100 yards).

Beers infused the practice of scientific play with order and efficiency, emphasizing aspirations of moral enrichment and patriotism propounded by Muscular Christianity, the philosophical linkage of athleticism, nationalism, manliness, discipline, and Christian faith articulated in England in the mid-nineteenth century.[32] "If our National game, while exercising the manly virtues, also trains the national and the moral, it will help to make us better men; and genuine 'pluck' will never go out of fashion in Canada."[33] Unlike baseball and cricket, which originated in the US and England, respectively, Beers viewed lacrosse as intrinsically Canadian, a natural resource along with timber, minerals, and wildlife, available for use by the land's newest inhabitants. He romanticized the sport's creators while relegating them to an inferior place in the Anglo social order. In 1880, Indigenous athletes effectively were barred from the organized sport ostensibly for their failure to conform to conventions of amateurism.[34] Despite the prohibitions, Indigenous communities found ways to use lacrosse as a vehicle to assert their culture and sovereignty.[35]

Profit-driven commercial interests compromised Beers's vision of lacrosse as a character-building and patriotic expression of Anglo-Canadian values, and the sport's popularity rose and fell over the years. At the time of Beers's death in 1900, the future of lacrosse was uncertain, but rule changes addressing safety, fair play, and making the game more legible for spectators contributed to its survival. Nearly one hundred years later, the Parliament of Canada passed the National Sports of Canada Act, which recognized lacrosse as the nation's summer sport along with hockey as the official winter sport.

Beers baked Anglo-Canadian values into his vision for the right way to play lacrosse. The slam dunk controversy in American collegiate basketball in the mid-twentieth century illustrates conflict in a well-established sport between conventional practice and a mode of play identified with an outsider group seeking to find their place in the game. The emphatic and often stylish exclamation of a player rising above the basket and stuffing the ball through the rim is now a signature move practiced by men and, increasingly, women. College and professional dunk contests are highlights of tournaments. From 1967 to 1976, however, the National Collegiate Athletic Association (NCAA) prohibited the dunk (as did high school associations), arguing that it was not a skillful shot, aesthetically; that it posed injury risks; and that it damaged backboards and rims, creating an unnecessary maintenance expense. Although players had dunked before and the propriety of the move had been a matter of debate since the 1930s (along with proposals to raise the height of the rim), many athletes and observers believed the NCAA's timing was based on more immediate concerns.[36] One was the overwhelming play under and above the basket of Kareem Abdul-Jabbar (then known as Lew Alcindor) at UCLA. This would not be the first instance of the game's administrators implementing a rule change intended to mitigate the impact of a dominant player, as we've seen in the histories of the key and three-point line. Another was the association of the dunk with Black streetball. Swirling in the subtext was the image of Black players dunking over and embarrassing white opponents and, furthermore, doing so with swagger that some administrators and coaches believed might alienate white spectators. In this view, Black players could have a place on NCAA courts, but the "white basketball unconscious," to use writer Yago Colás's term, of the sport's gatekeepers fostered a notion of the right way of play that dismissed the game many players had honed on urban courts in predominantly Black neighborhoods.[37] The dunk was, however, permitted in the professional game, and its acceptance there by fans and sponsors eventually led the NCAA to rescind the prohibition.

## UPENDING EXPECTATIONS

The spatial frame of the basketball court has always presented the potential for the dunk, but it had to be found by the players willing to expand the terms of right play. The Swedish artist Johan Ferner Ström has taken a very different approach. His interactive art installation *Puckelboll* (mogul ball), conceived in 2003, reimagines the familiar frame of soccer to encourage playful invention (figure 4.5). Versions have been realized in Malmö and Stockholm and proposed elsewhere. It transforms the level plane of the soccer pitch into a quirky undulating surface recalling moguls on a ski hill. Field markings, crisply rectangular on a soccer pitch, become squiggles, and whimsically shaped frames replace the orderly rectangles of traditional

Figure 4.5. Johan Ferner Ström, *Puckelboll*, interactive art installation, 2003; constructed in Kroksbäck Park, Malmö, Sweden, 2009. Photo by David Puig Serinyà. Courtesy of Johan Ferner Ström and David Puig Serinyà.

goals. The irregular terrain requires players to constantly adjust their footwork and respond to the ball's unanticipated trajectories. "Puckelboll," Ström writes, "is more similar [than a soccer pitch] to the playing field of life, which is in fact neither equilateral or uniform." "The unfairness of the field," he adds, "neutralizes the players' varying skill in terms of technology and strength. The injustices in the pitch make the game more fair in a strange way, which invites a more imaginative way of playing."[38] It prioritizes chance over predictability and displaces the ideal of consistency that underlies the frames of most field and court sports. Puckelboll is a field for play, not an organized sport, but unlike an undulating lawn, which has its own attractions for play, Ström's incorporation and deliberate distortion of the markings of soccer pitches marks it as a place to challenge conventions.

Practitioners of parkour and skateboarding frequently upend conventions of use, representation, and behavior by interrogating the purpose and material properties of features in the urban landscape built for very different uses. "Parkour," the scholars of urban studies Lieven Ameel and Sirpa Tani observe, "uses everyday environments in a unique way, which at the same time is unusual, spectacular and seemingly random, but also somehow ordinary, because most of the time *traceurs* [parkour practitioners] are simply practicing relatively easy and repetitive movement in nondescript environments."[39] For a parkour practitioner, a bench in a public plaza can be more than a place for sitting. It can be a thing to be vaulted, its seat and backrest beckoning as potential spring points for hands or feet. Similarly, "the skateboarders' reuse of the handrail," Borden writes, "ollieing onto the rail and, balanced perilously on the skateboard deck, sliding down the fulcrum line of the metal bar—targets something to do with safety and turns it into an object of risk. The whole logic of the handrail is turned on its head."[40] The shape of the railing, which we recognize through ordinary use as something to grip with the hand, presents the skateboarder with a surface for grinding. Such appropriations produce new, coterminous spatial constructions: the bench for sitting and vaulting, the railing for holding and sliding. "The bodily practice of parkour," Larsen writes, "is about *finding ever new ways to move* through urban space. This *search* is characterized by an intense bodily engagement and multisensory exploration of the material surroundings."[41] In so doing, she argues, practitioners circumvent the alienation of undifferentiated urban spaces by transforming them into places given meaning by their bodily experiences and stories.

While such reinterpretations can invigorate the monotony of an empty, windswept plaza, they also can spark conflicts over standards of decorum in and responsibility for the maintenance of shared public spaces. A person sipping a cup of coffee on a bench has a different appreciation of its shape, materials, and purpose than a parkour practitioner intent on performing a speed vault. Resolution of the competing claims can be difficult.

When the expectations of participants and witnesses are aligned, sporting events can take on collective spiritual meaning beyond the outcome of the game as expressions of lived religion (the spiritual and religious practice of laity outside religious institutions). Woodbine has experienced this in the street basketball tournaments held on public courts in Boston that bring players and spectators together to remember the victims of drugs and violence alongside enjoying the competition and festivities. Tournaments such as the Save R Streets Basketball Classic and the Russell Paulding Community Awareness Tournament are sites of community building and healing.

Woodbine describes how the courts manifest this social space as impromptu arenas. At the center, the familiar features (boundaries, center line and circle, the key and hoop at each end) frame the procedures of the game and afford the spontaneity of play. Loosely surrounding this setting are three rings of spectators. The outermost is the realm of gang members and hustlers. Composing the middle ring are casual fans, families, and players hanging out between games. Closest to the court, the elders of the game intently observe and comment on the action. Each group has its own preoccupations, but events on the court can bring them into alignment. "Street ball is rhythm and flow, and during its peak moments, the three rings of the asphalt collapse into a singular band, every head and toe pressed against the sidelines, caught up in the spectacle."[42] Woodbine likens the players to the Yoruba trickster god, Eshu, in their ability "to find a doorway on the basketball court that allowed them to slip between the present time and a time that is out of joint with everyday life on the streets."[43] Arising subjectively and precariously, these slippages can engage players and spectators as a community sharing moments of transcendent joy.

EPILOGUE

# BIG AIR

Soaring 24 feet, 4 inches above the deck of the halfpipe at the Genting Snow Park, north of Beijing, Japanese snowboarder Kaishu Hirano stretched his body into a backside air, arching his back, clasping the edge of his board with his right hand, and extending his left arm beyond his head (figure 5.1). For a few moments he flew at Olympic record height seemingly free of gravity—Superman on a snowboard. He returned to earth on the near wall of the pipe, crossed the floor, rode up the opposite wall, and took flight again. A crash on that landing ended his gold-medal hopes in the men's halfpipe competition at the 2022 Winter Olympics, but the fall did not tarnish the image of grace in the memories of the spectators in the stands and the millions of viewers watching on television and video streaming platforms. The medal winner was Kaishu's older brother, Ayumu, who thrilled judges, spectators, and fellow competitors by being the first in Olympic competition to land a frontside triple cork 1440 (four full rotations involving three flips) that he linked seamlessly with four other difficult tricks. He achieved big air as well, reaching a height of 18 feet, 1 inch above the deck (40 feet above the floor of the pipe). The day before, American rider Chloe Kim had won the gold medal in the women's halfpipe competition, flying 12 feet, 10 inches above the deck and executing five dazzling tricks in a creative display of technique and stylistic invention. These performances displayed mastery of the geometry of the venue's superpipe, a massive halfpipe of dense, artificial snow measuring more than 600 feet in length along an 18.2-degree slope with curved, 22-feet-high walls set 68 feet apart.

Figure 5.1. Kaishu Hirano, Men's Halfpipe Final, Beijing 2022 Winter Olympics, Genting Snow Park, Zhangjiakou, Hebei, China, February 11, 2022. MATSUO.K/AFLO SPORT/Alamy Live News.

Superpipe riding is an extreme sport of recent origin practiced by a small number of elite athletes but relatable to more casual snowboarders, skateboarders, and others attracted to the allure of catching big or big-seeming air off a bump or ramp. I'm a member of the latter category who has made only brief, very low-amplitude flights on skis off small moguls on Wisconsin ski hills, but those remarkably enduring memories from my youth are part of the embodied connection to what I see on the screen. The fundamental relationship between the architecture of the pipe and athletic performance, the primacy of televisual imagery to spectatorship, ethical questions raised by the pursuit of ever-bigger air, and halfpipe snowboarding's relatively recent development as an organized sport make it a useful example for recapitulating the themes of the architecture of the playing field that we've considered in the previous chapters.

Besides skis, people have contrived many ways of riding upright down snow-covered hills: on mono skis, cafeteria trays, slabs of wood, and other materials. A notable progenitor of the modern snowboard was the Snurfer, patented in 1968 by Sherman Poppen of Muskegon, Michigan, and marketed by Brunswick Corporation, a company better known as a maker of bowling equipment than of gear for snow sports. It recalled a large skateboard deck on which the rider stood sideways without bindings holding a short rope attached to the tip of the board. In his patent application, Poppen envisioned "a new winter sport, combining popular features of seashore surfing, skateboarding, and slalom water skiing."[1] Within a few years, other inventors and manufacturers offered variations that eliminated the rope, added metal edges and bindings, and improved the board's construction and behavior on the snow. The Snurfer gave way to the snowboard.

Poppen was prescient in anticipating the appeal of snowboarding to enthusiasts of surfing and skateboarding. Although many snowboarders enjoy cruising downhill on long runs and snowboard competitions include races modeled on ski events, the sport is known especially for the performance of the acrobatic tricks admired by skateboarders and surfers who were among the early adopters and brought their culture to the slopes.[2] They and their equipment met with an icy reception at most major ski resorts in the United States, but popular interest in the sport grew through savvy marketing by manufacturers and media companies capitalizing on the appeal of dazzling photographs of riders performing tricks against snowy backgrounds and blue sky. On the big screen, James Bond (doubled by the pioneering rider and manufacturer Tom Sims) eluded pursuers to the surf-song accompaniment of the Beach Boys in the 1985 film *A View to a Kill.* Sims, Jake Burton, and other manufacturers sponsored increasingly organized competitions throughout the 1980s, and in 1990 the International Federation of Snowboarding was founded to set standards and to prepare the path for recognition as an Olympic sport (the International Ski Federation took over governance in 2002).[3] Snowboard halfpipe events were introduced at the Winter X Games in 1997 and made their Olympic debut a year later in Nagano.

Even when allowed on ski hills, early snowboarders had to

find settings where they could develop their skills: they needed a downhill slope sufficiently pitched to maintain momentum without too much speed, the side of a conveniently shaped snowbank as a ramp for takeoffs, and, ideally, a run that was long enough to string together a series of hits (tricks) but that allowed social interaction among riders learning from each other. They sought equivalents to the flowing surfaces skateboarders enjoyed riding—the ramps and pipes in skateboard parks, the basins of unused swimming pools, and the giant pipes of water utility projects.[4] The development of the halfpipe as a frame for the emergent sport occurred alongside the efforts of riders to invent and master new skills. Both were informal processes of trial and error. In 1979, high school student Mark Anolik found a suitable natural equivalent on a slope at the edge of the refuse dump in Tahoe City, California. Wielding shovels and rakes, Anolik and his friends transformed this undefined location into a place given meaning by riders challenging each other to master tricks along and above the rough-hewn walls.

Sims was among those who found their way to the Tahoe City Pipe. He subsequently commissioned the construction of a halfpipe for the first Snowboard World Championships, held at Soda Springs, California, in 1983. The ambition exceeded the execution. Keith Kimmel, a leading rider at the time, recalled, "The pipe was horrible. It was basically two rows of snow chunks. And the chunks were only about four feet high."[5] When the competition moved to Breckenridge, Colorado, in 1986, the professional snowboarder Dave Alden and the resort's snow groomers achieved better results on a pipe measuring approximately 150 feet long and 60 feet wide with 5-foot-high walls. The following year they built a pipe that was 200 feet long, 40 feet wide with 6-foot-high walls. Greater length allows riders to perform more tricks on a run. Higher walls increase the riders' speed and the height to which they can soar. The relationship of height to width has implications for the radius shaping the walls.

Unlike skateboard halfpipes, which can be built as permanent installations or assembled when needed from prefabricated components, snowboard halfpipes depend on the vagaries of weather-dependent, wear-prone snow. Halfpipes can be carved out of huge piles of snow (as at the early pipes at Breckenridge) or built up from earthen channels that establish the overall dimension (as with today's largest pipes).[6] Pipe building evolved as a craft often involving riders as well as snow groomers and excavators. In the 1980s, builders used snowcats and other heavy machinery to push the snow into approximate arrangements but groomed the walls by hand. Snowboarder Kurt Heine developed specialized rakes and shovels to improve the efficiency and quality of this painstaking work, but mechanization was the key to building larger and more consistent pipes. In 1991, a skilled excavator named Lyle Blaisdell at Stratton Mountain in Vermont developed an attachment for his backhoe that allowed greater delicacy in trimming the walls and reduced the amount of hand labor. At the same time, an engineer and organic farmer in Colorado, Doug Waugh, applied his knowledge of grain augers and other agricultural machines to the problem and achieved a breakthrough that transformed pipe-building practices around the world.[7] His invention, the Pipe Dragon, has a curved arm that can make a continuous cut along the full height of the wall. It and the machines it inspired enabled the construction of pipes with higher walls and improved consistency, and reduced the time and cost of grooming. It was used to build the first Olympic halfpipe in Nagano, which had 11.5-foot-high walls set 49 feet apart and a run of 394 feet.

*Snowboarder* magazine assessed the state of halfpipe building in the run-up to the Nagano Olympics. The authors viewed inconsistency as a barrier to the growth of the sport but noted the promise of technological innovations like the Pipe Dragon and praised the efforts of regulatory bodies to develop standards. They also noted the tension that we have seen in the settings for other sports between the desires of athletes and regulators for uniformity and acceptance of variations due to local conditions: "The problem lies in the fact that too many people who control the decision-making process view the halfpipe as a fixed and static feature, and that once built, a pipe is left to the forces of nature. A severe change of opinion is needed, as the halfpipe needs to be thought of as an elastic form (almost lifelike) that changes daily and which needs continual maintenance." Despite these reservations, however, the future looked promising: "The halfpipe is part of snowboarding's unique culture. . . . The perfect halfpipe has yet to be built for snowboarders, but the time is close when all riders can have the same consistency in pipe shape and design from site to site."[8]

Unlike sports that established dimensional standards for playing fields with the intention that they would remain fixed despite changes in athletic performance, snowboard halfpipe riding did not retain the configuration at Nagano. Pipes grew larger to accommodate the increased skills of riders pursuing big air. For the 2002 Winter Olympics at Salt Lake City, the height of the walls increased to 18 feet with a corresponding increase of length. At Turin in 2006, the walls were 19 feet. Another big jump came with the 2010 Vancouver Olympics, where the walls increased to 22 feet, the height that has become the standard for today's superpipes (figure 5.2).

Larger pipes raise the stakes for athletes who must handle higher speeds and landings from greater heights and for

Figure 5.2. Queralt Castellet (*left*), Chloe Kim (*center*), and Sena Tomita (*right*), Women's Halfpipe Final, Beijing 2022 Winter Olympics, Genting Snow Park, Zhangjiakou, Hebei, China, February 10, 2022. PCN Photography/Alamy.

builders who face the technical and financial challenges of precisely constructing massive structures with snow. The safety of riders as well as their performance depends on the smoothness of the pipe. Snow must be consistent with respect to texture and surface, firm but soft enough for the snowboard edges to be effective. Surface blemishes, such as lumps or holes, can be disastrous, throwing riders off balance and precipitating dangerous crashes.[9]

Smoothness is a critical factor in the geometry of the pipe, and the profile of competition halfpipes is more complex than the semicircle the name suggests. From the top edge (the coping) down, the principal elements are a nearly vertical drop known as the vert, a curved transition, and the flat bottom linking the two walls, all running downhill on an 18-degree pitch. Elliptical transitions from floor to wall allow riders to maintain speed; achieve greater amplitude (bigger air); and reduce the forces of centripetal acceleration they experience at the bottom of the pipe, in the air above the pipe, and when landing on the walls. Recalling the increased radius of transitions introduced when the height of the walls increased from 12 to 15 feet (as at the 2000 US Open), the former champion rider (now commentator) Todd Richards observed, "It felt like you could just flow through the walls, instead of fighting to stay in the halfpipe and not flying into the middle of it."[10] Richards noted the importance of the interchange of builders and riders in making these refinements. Halfpipes have become engineered structures, but the craftspeople responsible for their construction and maintenance rely on feel alongside calculation. In an interview in *The Blade Dive*, a podcast devoted to snow sport industry operators and leaders, master halfpipe builder Jeremy Carpenter describes his near-meditative state at the controls of a Pipe Monster (a larger version of the Pipe Dragon, made by Zauug AG Eggiwil) sensing the smoothness of his cuts as well as relying on measured data.[11] He notes his preference for older pipe-shaping machines that are lighter and provide the operator with a more sensitive haptic response than heavier, more powerful newer models.

Snowboard halfpipes rarely exist in easily accessible locations, and their configurations are not audience friendly. Hardy fans who make it to the venues and find vantage points at the base of the pipe are rewarded more by the ambiance of the competition than by first-rate views of the action, which passes quickly and at a distance: a run down a 600-foot superpipe takes only twenty to thirty seconds. Spectators at the scene, like those watching remotely, rely on video coverage provided by camera operators in fixed positions and moving along the deck of the pipe with handheld equipment. Following a run, broadcast directors select appealing shots that focus on the rider and allow viewers to process the tricks in slow motion and from multiple camera angles. Spectators primarily know the sport from clips that frame the rider as a body in space flying free of earthly constraints. The architecture of the halfpipe falls away like a booster rocket after release of its payload.

In creating their repertoires of tricks, riders imaginatively build on their own skills and inspiration from the accomplishments of fellow snowboarders and skateboarders recorded by visual media, which have expanded from home movies and the photographs that were at the heart of early snowboarding magazines to commercial films and videos posted online. As with gymnastics skills, technical elements in figure skating, and skateboarding tricks, the names of snowboard tricks often commemorate their originators. The rotation known as the Cab, for instance, is named for a skateboard move introduced by Steve Caballero in 1981 and brought to snowboarding by Terry Kidwell three years later. Kidwell later adapted the McTwist, a flip and rotational combination created in 1984 by skateboarder Mike McGill. In 2010, Shaun White transformed the trick into the double McTwist 1260, combining an unprecedented three and a half rotations and two flips, an enduring signature move that other snowboarders struggled to emulate (figure 5.3).

Prior achievements are benchmarks for assessing innovation, a fundamental, performative aspect of the sport. The pipe defines boundaries and imposes direction, but it is up to the riders to determine how they negotiate it. "You're able to separate yourself from the competition by being yourself, by doing something different or unique, or something just speaks to you personally," Chase Josey observes in a video produced by

Figure 5.3. Composite image showing Shaun White executing a backside double McTwist 1260 at the PyeongChang 2018 Winter Olympics, Bogwang Phoenix Park, PyeongChang, South Korea, February 14, 2018. Bedel Saget and Jeremy White/*The New York Times*/Redux.

the International Olympic Committee (IOC).[12] Maddie Mastro explains, "When I'm in the air and am going big, there's not a lot going through your head other than what you're doing, and it's just this peaceful floating feeling that you know what you're doing, and your body is performing it perfectly." Her statement expresses her aesthetic engagement fully immersed in awareness of her body, the board, and the forces arising from her encounter with the geometry of the pipe. Another rider (and musician), Pat Burgener, contributes, "It's about getting the right rhythm." These statements remind me of an observation by the choreographer Merce Cunningham: "When I dance, it means: this is what I am doing." He added, "This is not a feeling about something, this is a whipping of the mind and body into an action that is so intense, that for the brief moment involved, the mind and body are one."[13]

Looking beyond rhythmic movement's physiological mechanics, philosophers have explored its centrality to the embodied experience of aesthetic engagement. "The repetitions and redundancies of rhythms, their symmetries and asymmetries, interact in ways that cannot be reduced to the discrete and fixed determination of analytic thought."[14] Henri Lefebvre wrote this with music and dance in mind, but his observation also pertains to rhythms in the spatial practices of sport. The philosopher of sport Sigmund Loland has taken up this theme as it applies to snowboarding. His insights allow us to frame the observations of Mastro and Burgener in phenomenological terms: "Rhythm is understood as qualitative characteristics of movement patterns that are more than the mere sum of their parts: they are holistic entities that can only be rendered meaningful as experiential wholes. In successful rides, snowboarders do not 'have' a body, rather they 'are' their bodies."[15]

The quest for innovation fueled by riders' competitive spirit and the desire of sponsors and broadcasters to attract viewers has inspired superpipes and jaw-dropping tricks but increased risk. Olympic bronze medalist Kelly Clark recalls, "When things switched to the 22-foot wall, the entire way you rode a halfpipe really changed. It was a real dividing point in the sport where it really stopped one entire generation, and a new generation started from 2010. . . . The fundamental aspects of the sport changed dramatically."[16] As riders have found new, faster lines down and across the pipe to achieve the height and hang time necessary for the performance of more rotations and inversions, they have had to manage fear.[17] The death of champion freestyle skier Sarah Burke on a 22-foot halfpipe in Utah in 2012 underscored the risks throughout the tightly knit community of pipe riders.[18] It also points to ethical considerations that reach beyond the internal culture of the sport.

Like athletes in other physically demanding sports, freestyle snowboard riders and skiers accept the inevitability of non-life-threatening injuries in training and competition. Spectators, as well, grant the risk as part of the game, but there is an ill-defined line separating toleration and recognition that the performative expectations of a sport are too dangerous. I noted in chapter 3 the example of American football banning the brutal flying-wedge running formation in 1905. Assessment of the risks of concussions in football and other sports today remains unresolved. Alongside scientific findings, these decisions involve social accord of practitioners and spectators. For snowboarding and freestyle skiing, the 22-foot halfpipe is the current standard for the Olympics and other major competitions, but it may be subject to revision as freestyle snowboarding and skiing evolve. Pipes could continue to become larger as athletes pursue bigger air, or they could be superseded by other competition formats to accommodate reassessment of athletic challenges, safety, and shifts of popular interest among spectators and sponsors. The modified halfpipe event, for instance, which tests a variety of skills evoking the sport's origins, presents riders with a new laboratory for spatial invention.[19]

With this, we'll leave the wintry realm of snowboarding and return to the observation by Krakauer regarding sports as an expression of human predilection as "complexity makers and complexity detectors."[20] Both parts of the phrase are evident in the many permutations of playing fields and the performances they enable. Playing fields tangibly frame their respective sports by demarcating boundaries and orienting movement within. The settings for some sports, such as a surf break or the route of an urban parkour course, involve minimal intrusion on a natural site or city neighborhood; others require varying degrees of construction, from setting up cones to mark the corners of a soccer pitch in a park to shaping two hundred acres of land for a golf course. They all have characteristic spatial properties and histories that include the social context of their origins and the roles of the people who build, maintain, or otherwise designate their use for sport. Backyard hockey rinks, rural baseball diamonds, urban basketball courts, and hand-dug halfpipes have their place alongside their more glamourous collegiate and professional counterparts as works of architecture and landscape architecture.

The settings for sport are performance sites. Like an empty stage, building, or city park, they come to life when occupied by players and spectators. Intertwined with the tactics drawn up to take advantage of the possibilities afforded by the settings is the embodied engagement of players who experience the flow of the game relationally. Particularly in sports contested head-to-head, players employ feints and formations intended to influence their opponents' perception of the field. Perception of the action by spectators and athletes alike also can be reframed spatially and temporally by televisual and other media.

For the duration of a game, players, officials, and spectators occupy a performative space—Huizinga's magic circle—that operates under the special rules and rituals of the sport but remains embedded within larger social structures. While we can approach sporting events from the perspective of wins, losses, and the metrics of athletic achievement, we also can take pleasure in them as sites of spatial exploration. Athletes, like dancers, architects, and other designers of the built environment, distill ways of engaging the world around us.

# ACKNOWLEDGMENTS

This book has its origins in spirited conversations with students in the School of Architecture at the University of Texas at Austin (UTSOA) and the School of Architecture at Carnegie Mellon University that raised intertwining questions about sports architecture—buildings and landscapes—and the architecture inherent in sports—embedded in rules and emergent in play. The spur to build on these informal discussions came from the long-running British Studies seminar (now Program in British, Irish, and Empire Studies) at the University of Texas at Austin led by Wm. Roger Louis. It was an inspiring, if seemingly unlikely, fit. The participants represented a variety of interests and urged me to frame my topic broadly. Further encouragement came from my colleagues in the UTSOA, including Michael Benedikt, Juan Miró, and Allan Shearer. Elsewhere on campus, Jan Todd welcomed me to the H. J. Lutcher Stark Center for Physical Culture and Sports, which she directs, and made introductions to Tolga Ozyurtcu, the center's assistant director, and Thomas Hunt, editor for the Terry and Jan Todd Series on Physical Culture and Sports. Nancy Levenson, editor of *Places Journal*, and Sonja Dümpelmann, convener of the Dumbarton Oaks symposium *Landscape, Sport, Environment*, guided publication of preliminary studies. I was delighted to become acquainted with the International Association for the Philosophy of Sport and have learned much from Kenneth Aggerholm, Signe Højbjerre Larsen, Sigmund Loland, and other members. The Cooperstown Symposium on Baseball and American Culture was a receptive and informative venue for my thoughts on the spatial properties of diamonds and strike zones. Caroline Stacey, now an architect of professional sports facilities, assisted my research while a student at the UTSOA. Anna Andrzejewski and Samuel Dodd gave incisive readings to the manuscript at critical points in its development. The artist Johan Ferner Fencer Ström responded generously to my inquiries. Holly Buechel, Barbara Buenger, Stefani Danes, and Janet Kennedy shared their expertise. At the University of Texas Press, I have benefitted from the knowledge and skills of former editor-in-chief Dawn Durante, current editor-in-chief Casey Kittrell, acquisitions editor Sarah McGavick, editorial assistant Mia Uribe-Kozlovsky, manuscript editor Lynne Ferguson, and copy editor Sarah Hudgens. I was the beneficiary of perceptive criticism by the anonymous scholars who reviewed the manuscript. Among the libraries without which this book would not be possible, I owe special thanks to the University of Texas Libraries and the University of Wisconsin–Madison Libraries, which provided essential services throughout the recent pandemic. The Department of Art History at the University of Wisconsin–Madison has generously provided me with an academic anchor on that great campus. Today, more than ever, local public libraries merit recognition, and I've been fortunate to live a short bike ride from the Mead Public Library in Sheboygan, Wisconsin. Alongside the many programs the small staff offers to all comers in the community is an excellent interlibrary loan service, portal to a vast and necessary world of print sources. My family has contributed more than encouragement and forbearance. My children—Patrick Cleary; Amanda Cleary; her wife, Abbey Patteson; my stepdaughter, Helen Larsen; and her husband, Joshua Sayre—have shared their experiences on sports fields and, in Helen's case, the dance studio. For my wife, Sarah Cleary, this project has been a bit like an uninvited, overstaying guest, but her sharp eye, open ears, forthright criticism, and good will have enriched it, and my life, in countless ways.

# NOTES

INTRODUCTION

1. John Krakauer and Patrick Vieira, "Keeping Your Eye on the Ball," New York City Football Club, April 2017, SoundCloud audio, https://soundcloud.com/nycfc/patrick-vieira-john-krakauer-keeping-your-eye-on-the-ball. See also Zach Schonbrun, *The Performance Cortex: How Neuroscience Is Redefining Athletic Genius* (New York: Dutton, 2018), 116–117.

2. Bernard Suits, "The Elements of Sport," in *The Philosophy of Sport: A Collection of Original Essays*, ed. Robert G. Osterhoudt (Springfield, IL: Thomas, 1973), 55.

3. R. Scott Kretchmar, "Game Flaws," *Journal of the Philosophy of Sport* 32, no. 1 (2005): 43–44.

4. See Howard Shubert, *Architecture on Ice: A History of the Hockey Arena* (Montreal: McGill-Queen's University Press, 2016); Benjamin D. Lisle, *Modern Coliseum: Stadiums and American Culture* (Philadelphia: University of Pennsylvania Press, 2017); Benjamin S. Flowers, *Sport and Architecture* (Milton Park, UK: Routledge, 2017); Paul Goldberger, *Ballpark: Baseball in the American City* (New York: Alfred A. Knopf, 2019).

5. Karl Ove Knausgaard, *Autumn* (New York: Penguin, 2017), 45.

6. Louis Kahn, "Architecture Is the Thoughtful Making of Spaces," *Perspecta*, no. 4 (1957): 2–3.

7. Geoffrey Scott, *The Architecture of Humanism: A Study in the History of Taste* (London: Constable and Company, 1914), 213, 227.

8. Bernard Tschumi, Omar Khan, and Dorita Hannah, "Performance/Architecture: An Interview with Bernard Tschumi," *Journal of Architectural Education* 61, no. 4 (2008): 53.

9. Arnold Berleant, *Art and Engagement* (Philadelphia: Temple University Press, 1991), 77. Emphasis in original.

10. Kent C. Bloomer, Charles W. Moore, and Robert J. Yudell, *Body, Memory, and Architecture* (New Haven, CT: Yale University Press, 1977), 56–75.

11. Harry Francis Mallgrave, *Architecture and Embodiment: The Implications of the New Sciences and Humanities for Design* (London: Routledge, 2013), 137.

12. Eduardo Galeano, *Soccer in Sun and Shadow*, trans. Mark Fried, 2nd paperback ed. (London: Verso, 2003), 82.

13. For other instances of soccer players in Soviet Russian art, see Przemyslaw Strozek, "Footballers in Avant-Garde Art and Socialist

Realism before World War II," in *Handbuch der Sportgeschicte Osteuropas*, ed. Anke Hilbrenner, Ekaterina Emeliantseva, Christian Koller, Manfred Zeiler, and Stefan Zwicker (Bonn: Universität Bonn, 2015).

14. Le Corbusier, *The City of To-morrow and Its Planning*, trans. Frederick Etchells (New York: Payson & Clarke, 1929), 23, 24.

15. For a discussion of Le Corbusier's use of this image, see Bernard Vere, *Sport and Modernism in the Visual Arts in Europe* (Manchester, UK: Manchester University Press, 2018), 62ff.

16. Camilla Ghisleni, "What Is Hedonistic Sustainability in Architecture?," ArchDaily, September 4, 2023, https://www.archdaily.com/1006443/what-is-hedonistic-sustainability-in-architecture.

17. For a discussion on sport and dance, see Jason Holt, *Kinetic Beauty: The Philosophical Aesthetics of Sport* (Abingdon, UK: Routledge, 2020), 109–119.

18. Twyla Tharp, *Dance Is a Man's Sport, Too*, performed on *Omnibus*, ABC Television, 1980, Twyla Tharp Dance Foundation, New York, https://www.twylatharp.org/works/dance-mans-sport-too.

19. For a summary of contested positions, see Holt, *Kinetic Beauty*, 99–108.

20. For my initial explorations of this topic, see "Well Played! An Architectural View of Sports," in *Resplendent Adventures with Britannia: Personalities, Politics and Culture in Britain*, ed. Wm. Roger Louis (London and Austin, TX: I. B. Tauris and Harry Ransom Center, 2015); "The Architecture of Sports," *Places Journal*, July 2017, https://doi.org/10.22269/170725; "Fields of Play: Laboratories of Spatial Invention," in *Landscapes for Sport: Histories of Exercise, Sport, and Health*, ed. Sonja Dümpelmann (Washington, DC: Dumbarton Oaks Research Library and Collection, 2022).

## CHAPTER 1. FRAMES

1. Suits, "The Elements of Sport," 55.

2. Knausgaard, *Autumn*, 45.

3. For a critical study of stadia design in the late-twentieth and twenty-first centuries, see Benjamin Flowers, *Beautiful Moves: Designing Stadia* (London: Lund Humphries, 2018).

4. James Herbert, "NBA to Use Interactive LED Glass Court at 2024 All-Star Weekend: Here's How 'Huge Television Screen' Will Work," CBS Sports, February 5, 2024, https://www.cbssports.com/nba/news/nba-to-use-interactive-led-glass-court-at-2024-all-star-weekend-heres-how-huge-television-screen-will-work/; John Breech, "NFL Gets Thrown under the Bus for Slippery Super Bowl Field Conditions That One Player Called the 'Worst' Ever," CBS Sports, February 16, 2023, https://www.cbssports.com/nfl/news/nfl-gets-thrown-under-the-bus-for-slippery-super-bowl-field-conditions-that-one-player-called-the-worst-ever/.

5. David Adler, in discussion with the author, May 10, 2022.

6. For examples of the playing fields of amateur soccer in Europe, see

Marta Kurkowska-Budzan, "Wild Stadia: Vernacular Sport Spaces in the Polish Countryside during the Socialist Era," in *Landscapes for Sport: Histories of Physical Exercise, Sport, and Health*, ed. Sonja Dümpelmann (Washington, DC: Dumbarton Oaks, 2022); Hans van der Meer, "European Fields: The Landscape of Lower League Football," in *Landscapes for Sport*, ed. Sonja Dümpelmann (Washington, DC: Dumbarton Oaks, 2022); Hans van der Meer, *European Fields: The Landscape of Lower League Football* (London: SteidlMack, 2006).

7. John Bale, "Space, Place and Body Culture: Yi-Fu Tuan and a Geography of Sport," *Geografiska Annaler. Series B, Human Geography* 78, no. 3 (1996): 165.

8. John Bale, *Sports Geography*, 2nd ed. (London: Routledge, 2003), chap. 7; John Bale, *Landscapes of Modern Sport* (Leicester: Leicester University Press, 1994), chap. 3.

9. William George Beers, *Lacrosse: The National Game of Canada* (Montreal: Dawson Brothers, 1869), 54.

10. John Thorn, "The Game That Got Away," *Our Game*, MLB.com /BLOGS, July 3, 2012, https://ourgame.mlblogs.com/the-game-that-got-away-a385699cd936.

11. The rules published in 1845 by New York's Knickerbocker Base Ball Club specified the distance between bases as 42 paces, which allowed for variation depending on the stride of the person laying out the field. The unit of measurement was changed to feet in 1857. Peter Morris, "1.16 Ninety Feet," in *A Game of Inches: The Stories behind the Innovations That Shaped Baseball*, 2nd rev. ed. (Chicago: Ivan R. Dee, 2010), 26.

12. Mike Thomas, "The Sodfather," *Smithsonian Magazine*, April 2008, https://www.smithsonianmag.com/arts-culture/the-sodfather-31895138/; Morris, *Game of Inches*, 330–331.

13. George F. Will, *Men at Work: The Craft of Baseball* (New York: Harper, 1991), 267–268.

14. The implications of the siting of MLB ballparks on the shape of the outfield are addressed in Goldberger, *Ballpark*.

15. Roger Angell, *The Summer Game* (New York: Viking Press, 1972), 73. Quoted in Goldberger, *Ballpark*, 179.

16. Tom Shieber, "The Evolution of the Baseball Diamond: Perfection Came Slowly," *Baseball Research Journal* 23 (1994): 4–7, Society for American Baseball Research, https://sabr.org/journal/article/the-evolution-of-the-baseball-diamond-perfection-came-slowly/.

17. Henry Chadwick, ed., *Spalding's Official Base Ball Guide*, vol. 1900 (New York: American Sports Publishing Company, 1900), 174, 201.

18. "Satchel Paige Quotes," Baseball Almanac, accessed July 31, 2023, https://www.baseball-almanac.com/quotes/quopaig.shtml.

19. Will, *Men at Work*, 243. See also Roger Angell, "Distance: The Game Belongs to Bob Gibson," *New Yorker*, September 22, 1980, https://www.newyorker.com/magazine/1980/09/22/distance.

20. "1-11 Strike Zone," in Morris, *Game of Inches*, 20–21.

21. Major League Baseball, *Official Baseball Rules* (New York: Office of the Commisioner of Baseball, 2021), 152, 162.

22. Zach Helfand, "Kill the Umpire," *New Yorker*, August 30, 2021.

23. The geometry of the diamond does not dictate the counterclockwise route base runners must follow. In forerunners of baseball, such as rounders, base runners sometimes ran clockwise. Softball in 1908 permitted the leadoff hitter to choose the direction to be run. Baseball historians speculate that the convention of counterclockwise movement relates to throwing and batting preferences. See "1.7 Running Counterclockwise," in Morris, *Game of Inches*, 15–16; and John Schwartz, "Baseball: The Counterclockwise Sport," *Baseball Research Journal* (1978), Society for American Baseball Research, https://sabr.org/journal/article/baseball-the-counterclockwise-sport/.

24. Gary Belsky and Neil Fine, *On the Origins of Sports: The Early History and Original Rules of Everybody's Favorite Games* (New York: Artisan, 2016), 159.

25. For a discussion of aesthetic and ethical aspects of this and other legal time-wasting tactics, see Kretchmar, "Game Flaws."

26. For an account of the deliberations underlying these innovations, see Roger R. Tamte, *Walter Camp and the Creation of American Football* (Urbana: University of Illinois Press, 2018), 42–60.

27. Tamte, *Walter Camp and the Creation of American Football*, 56.

28. World Squash Federation, *Specifications for Squash Courts*, (Hastings, UK: World Squash Federation, 2013), https://www.worldsquash.org/wp-content/uploads/2021/08/171128 Court-Specifications.pdf.

29. James Zug, *Squash: A History of the Game* (New York: Scribner, 2003).

30. Zug, *Squash*, 18–20.

31. Zug, *Squash*, 35–39.

32. Zug, *Squash*, 165–166.

33. "Pro Squash Is Taking Its Court on the Road," *New York Times*, November 9, 1984, section B, https://www.nytimes.com/1984/11/09/sports/pro-squash-is-taking-its-court-on-the-road.html.

34. For a concise account of the sport from the point of view of cultural geography, see Thomas J. Baerwald, "Basketball," in *The Theater of Sport*, ed. Karl B. Raitz (Baltimore: Johns Hopkins University Press, 1995).

35. James Naismith, "Basketball: Its Origin and Development," in *Basketball: Great Writing about America's Game*, ed. Alexander Wolff (New York: Library of America, 2018), 5.

36. Luther Gulick, ed., *Official Basket Ball Rules as Adopted by the Young Men's Christian Association Athletic League of North America*, Spalding's Athletic Library: Official Basket Ball Guide, Season 1896–1897 (New York: American Sports Publishing Company, 1896), 34.

37. Robert W. Peterson, "When the Court Was a Cage," *Sports Illustrated*, November 11, 1991, https://vault.si.com/vault/1991/11/11/when

-the-court-was-a-cage-in-the-early-days-of-pro-basketball-the-players-were-segregated-from-the-fans.

38. Quoted in Robert Allen Cherry, *Wilt: Larger than Life* (Chicago: Triumph Books, 2004), 146.

39. Robert Feinberg, "Does Moving the NBA 3-Point Line Help Good 3-Point Shooting Teams?," Harvard Sports Analysis Collective, (blog), May 31, 2017, http://harvardsportsanalysis.org/2017/05/does-moving-the-nba-3-point-line-help-good-3-point-shooting-teams/.

40. Jeff Zillgitt, "Things We'd Change in Sports: Expand the NBA Court to Accommodate Bigger, Faster Players," *USA Today*, March 9, 2019, https://www.usatoday.com/story/sports/nba/columnist/jeff-zillgitt/2019/03/09/expand-nba-court-improve-flow/3070024002/.

41. Kenneth I. Helphand, "Learning from Linksland," *Landscape Journal* 14, no. 1 (Spring 1995).

42. H. N. Wethered and T. Simpson, *The Architectural Side of Golf* (London: Longmans, Green, and Co., 1929), 2.

43. Wethered and Simpson, *The Architectural Side of Golf*, 58.

44. Ben Crenshaw and Melanie Hauser, *A Feel for the Game: To Brookline and Back* (New York: Doubleday, 2001), xii.

45. For an introduction to these approaches to hole design, see Tom Doak, *The Anatomy of a Golf Course* (New York: Lyons and Burford, 1992), 66; Robert Trent Jones Jr., *Golf by Design: How to Lower Your Score by Reading the Features of a Course* (Boston: Little, Brown and Company, 1993).

46. Mike McAllister, "Pete Dye: The Genius Who Loathed Plans," PGA Tour, March 8, 2020, https://www.pgatour.com/long-form/2020/03/08/pete-dye-genius-course-design-tpc-sawgrass-the-players-championship.html.

47. Alister MacKenzie, *The Spirit of St. Andrews* (Chelsea, MI: Sleeping Bear Press, 1995), 51.

48. MacKenzie included this point among his criteria for an ideal golf course. See MacKenzie, *Spirit of St. Andrews*, 42.

49. Doak, *Anatomy of a Golf Course*, 42.

50. Doak, *Anatomy of a Golf Course*, 37–39.

51. For a summary of MacKenzie's experience as a camoufleur, see Tom Doak, James S. Scott, and Raymund M. Haddock, *The Life and Work of Dr. Alister MacKenzie* (Chelsea, MI: Sleeping Bear Press, 2001), 38–45.

52. MacKenzie, *Spirit of St. Andrews*, 264.

53. Alister MacKenzie, "Entrenchment and Camouflage," *Professional Memoires, Corps of Engineers, United States Army, and Engineer Department at Large* 9, no. 47 (September–October 1917).

54. Alister MacKenzie, "Common Sense of Camouflage Defense," *The Military Engineer* 26, no. 145 (January–February 1934): 42–43.

55. MacKenzie, *Spirit of St. Andrews*, 265.

CHAPTER 2. MEDIATED SPACE

1. John Thorn, "The New York Clipper and Sporting Weeklies of Its Time," *Our Game*, MLB.com/BLOGS, February 20, 2017, https://ourgame.mlblogs.com/the-new-york-clipper-and-sporting-weeklies-of-its-time-b343de7f474f.

2. "Baseball: The Professional Arena," *Brooklyn Daily Eagle* (Brooklyn, NY), June 1, 1875, https://bklyn.newspapers.com/image/50419715/. Emphasis in original.

3. Ted Patterson, *The Golden Voices of Baseball* (Champaign, IL: Sports Publishing, 2002), 12–17.

4. Audrey Adams, "Radio Football down the Years," BBC, January 14, 2002, https://news.bbc.co.uk/sport2/hi/football/1760579.stm.

5. Bill Mercer, *Play-by-Play: Tales from a Sportscasting Insider* (New York: First Taylor Trade Publishing, 2007), 141.

6. Mercer, *Play-by-Play*, 153.

7. Gaston Bachelard, *The Poetics of Space*, trans. Maria Jolas (Boston: Beacon Press, 1969), 6.

8. Gary Berman, "The First Olympics on Television (It Wasn't in the U.S.)," Medium, July 22, 2021, https://garryberman.medium.com/the-first-olympics-broadcast-on-television-it-wasnt-in-the-u-s-519190ed83fa.

9. Scott Murray, "How Arsenal Blazed TV Trail, Jostling for Airtime with Cartoons and Smut," *Guardian*, September 16, 2015, https://www.theguardian.com/football/tvandradioblog/2015/sep/16/how-arsenal-blazed-tv-trail-jostling-for-airtime-with-cartoons-and-smut.

10. James R. Walker and Robert V. Bellamy Jr., *Center Field Shot: A History of Baseball on Television* (Lincoln: University of Nebraska Press, 2008), 6–10.

11. Ken Kerschbaumer, "World Series 2023: Drones Are Set to Fly for Fox Sports' Coverage," *SVG News*, October 27, 2023, https://www.sportsvideo.org/2023/10/27/drones-set-to-fly-for-fox-sports-world-series-coverage/.

12. For an account of the production of NBC's *Sunday Night Football*, see Jody Rosen, "Behind the Scenes of the Most Spectacular Show on TV," *New York Times*, December 2, 2023, https://www.nytimes.com/2023/12/02/magazine/sunday-night-football.html.

13. MLB Vault, "1952 World Series, Game 7: Yankees @ Dodgers," YouTube video, September 16, 2010, https://www.youtube.com/watch?v=hqZnPQnxO9U&t=1428s.

14. "WS1960 Gm 7: Mazeroski Hits a Walk-off Homer in Game 7," posted November 1, 2016, by MLB, YouTube, 1:45, https://www.youtube.com/watch?v=A-OCXYjVL4U.

15. Lawrence Mullen, "Joe Aceti on Sports Television Directing," University of Nevada, Las Vegas, https://lmullen.faculty.unlv.edu/vita.2/aceti.bio.htm.

16. Mullen, "Joe Aceti on Sports Television Directing," 22.

17. Garry Whannel, *Fields in Vision: Television Sports and Cultural Transformation* (London: Routledge, 1992).

18. Whannel, *Fields in Vision*, 94.

19. Tim Dant, *Television and the Moral Imaginary: Society through the Small Screen* (Houndmills, UK: Palgrave Macmillan, 2012), 104.

20. Eric S. Hintz, "The Invention of Instant Replay," Lemelson Center for the Study of Invention and Innovation, Smithsonian Institution, January 20, 2022, https://invention.si.edu/invention-instant-replay; Ray Gamache, *A History of Sports Highlights: Replayed Plays from Edison to ESPN* (Jefferson, NC: McFarland and Company, 2010), 118.

21. Jane Feuer, "The Concept of Live Television: Ontology as Ideology," in *Regarding Television: Critical Approaches—An Anthology*, ed. E. Ann Kaplan (Frederick, MD: University Publications of America, 1983), 15.

22. Feuer, "The Concept of Live Television," 16.

23. Christopher Hanson, "The Instant Replay: Time and Time Again," *Spectator* [USC] 28, no. 2 (Fall 2008): 51–60.

24. David Best, *Philosophy and Human Movement* (London: George Allen & Unwin, 1978), 108; Holt, *Kinetic Beauty*, 92.

25. Whannel, *Fields in Vision*, 98.

26. Lisle, *Modern Coliseum*, 243–244.

27. Harry Collins, "The Philosophy of Umpiring and the Introduction of Decision-Aid Technology," *Journal of the Philosophy of Sport* 37, no. 2 (2010): 135–146.

28. Bill Pennington and Karen Crouse, "Attention, Second-Guessers: Golf Takes Calls (and Texts)," *New York Times*, April 13, 2013, https://www.nytimes.com/2013/04/14/sports/golf/television-viewers-flag-rule-violations-as-golf-officials-take-note.html.

29. Greg Garber, "Jumbotron: The Big Picture," ESPN, http://www.espn.com/nfl/feature/featureVideo?page=jumbotron.

30. Mihaly Csikszentmihalyi, *Flow: The Psychology of Optimal Experience* (New York: HarperCollins, 1990).

31. Garber, "Jumbotron."

32. Gabriel Fernandez, "LOOK: Oklahoma State Displays Yellow Lines on Video Board to Distract Texas Kicker's Field Goal Attempt," CBS Sports, October 31, 2020, https://www.cbssports.com/college-football/news/look-oklahoma-state-displays-yellow-lines-on-video-board-to-distract-texas-kickers-field-goal-attempt/.

33. Neil Vigdor, "The Houston Astros' Cheating Scandal: Sign-Stealing, Buzzer Intrigue and Tainted Pennants," *New York Times*, July 16, 2020, https://www.nytimes.com/article/astros-cheating.html; Jonathan Silverman, ed., *Astros and Asterisks: Houston's Sign-Stealing Scandal Explained* (Austin: University of Texas Press, 2023).

34. Iain Borden, *Skateboarding, Space and the City* (Oxford, UK: Berg, 2001), 123.

35. Borden, *Skateboarding, Space and the City*, 120.

36. Borden, *Skateboarding, Space and the City*, 122.

37. Borden, *Skateboarding, Space and the City*, 91.

38. Borden, *Skateboarding, Space and the City*, 114–116.

39. Andy Miah, *Sport 2.0: Transforming Sports for a Digital World* (Cambridge, MA: MIT Press, 2017), 108.

40. An extension of this trend of increased viewer interaction is the Fan Controlled Football League, which allows subscribers to participate in crowdsourced decisions regarding lineups and even real-time play calling during games. See https://www.fcf.io.

41. Miah, *Sport 2.0*, 109.

42. Walker and Bellamy, *Center Field Shot*, 300–303.

43. Jacob Stern, "A Fake Yellow Line Changed Football Forever," *Atlantic*, February 8, 2024, https://www.theatlantic.com/technology/archive/2024/02/football-virtual-yellow-line-augmented-reality/677384/.

44. Eric Lang, "Analyzing the Strike Zone as a Three-Dimensional Volume," Hardball Times, September 14, 2015, https://tht.fangraphs.com/analyzing-the-strike-zone-as-a-three-dimensional-volume/.

45. Helfand, "Kill the Umpire."

46. Seth Stevenson, "The Man Who Saved Tennis," Slate, November 6, 2012, https://slate.com/culture/2012/11/hawk-eye-saved-tennis-from-bad-line-calls-paul-hawkins-invention-designed-for-cricket-has-moved-to-other-sports.html.

47. Andrew Keh, "We Hope Your Cheers for This Article Are for Real," *New York Times*, June 17, 2020, https://www.nytimes.com/2020/06/16/sports/coronavirus-stadium-fans-crowd-noise.html; Emma Baccellieri, "What's behind MLB's Fake Crowd Noise? A Conductor With an iPad," *Sports Illustrated*, September 5, 2020, https://www.si.com/mlb/2020/09/05/baseball-fake-crowd-nosie.

48. Juhani Pallasmaa, *The Eyes of the Skin: Architecture and the Senses* (Chichester, UK: John Wiley & Sons, 2005), 49.

49. For an overview of the topic of sound in sport venues, see Bale, *Landscapes of Modern Sport*, 139–141. On hockey arenas, see Shubert, *Architecture on Ice*, 209. On basketball arenas, see Alan Schwarz, "Stoking Excitement, Arenas Pump Up the Volume," *New York Times*, June 6, 2011, https://www.nytimes.com/2011/06/07/sports/basketball/stoking-fans-excitement-arenas-pump-up-the-volume.html.

50. Nick Greene, "Is CBS Piping Fake Birds into Its Masters Coverage?," Slate, April 12, 2019, https://slate.com/culture/2019/04/masters-cbs-coverage-birds-real-fake.html.

51. Chuck Quirmbach, "Thousands of Recorded Voices Will Cheer Milwaukee Brewers at Miller Park," WUWM 89.7, July 24, 2020, https://www.wuwm.com/post/thousands-recorded-voices-will-cheer-milwaukee-brewers-miller-park#stream/0.

52. Miah, *Sport 2.0*, 120.

CHAPTER 3. LABORATORIES OF SPATIAL INVENTION

1. Steven J. Jackson and Brendan Hokowhitu, "Sport, Tribes, and Technology: The New Zealand All Blacks Haka and the Politics of Identity," *Journal of Sport and Social Issues* 26, no. 2 (2002): 125–139.

2. Berleant, *Art and Engagement*, 158.

3. For more on these themes, see Holt, *Kinetic Beauty*; Stephen D. Mumford, *Watching Sport: Aesthetics, Ethics and Emotion*, Ethics and Sport (Hoboken: Taylor & Francis, 2011); Hans Ulrich Gumbrecht, *In Praise of Athletic Beauty* (Cambridge, MA: Harvard University Press, 2006).

4. Johan Huizinga, *Homo Ludens: A Study of the Play-Element in Culture*, trans. R. F. C. Hull (London: Routledge & Kegan Paul, 1949), 10.

5. Katie Salen Tekinbaş and Eric Zimmerman, *Rules of Play: Game Design Fundamentals* (Cambridge, MA: MIT Press, 2003), 94–99; Ian Bogost, *Play Anything: The Pleasure of Limits, the Uses of Boredom, and the Secret of Games* (New York: Basic Books, 2016), 107–110.

6. Huizinga, *Homo Ludens*, 10.

7. James R. Hines, *Figure Skating: A History* (Urbana: University of Illinois Press and World Figure Skating Museum and Hall of Fame, 2006).

8. Montagu S. Monier-Williams, Winter Randell Pidgeon, and Arthur Dryden, *Figure Skating Simple and Combined; Being an Enlarged Edition of "Combined Figure-Skating" Arranged as a Complete Text-Book of the Art of Skating as Practised in the Leading Skating Clubs of Great Britain* (London: Horace Cox, 1892).

9. ABC Sports television coverage of the 1984 Winter Olympics held in Sarajevo included a concise introduction to the compulsory figures competition featuring demonstrations by champion skater Scott Hamilton; see https://www.youtube.com/watch?v=jU9Hy1upUro.

10. David Winner, *Brilliant Orange: The Neurotic Genius of Dutch Soccer* (Woodstock, NY: Overlook Press, 2002), 46–47.

11. Jonathan Wilson, *Inverting the Pyramid: A History of Football Tactics* (London: Orion, 2008), 12–20.

12. David Goldblatt, *The Ball Is Round: A Global History of Football* (New York: Riverhead Books, 2008), 36.

13. Wilson, *Inverting the Pyramid*, 15–17.

14. A pioneer adopting new approaches to player positioning in response to the revised offside rule was Herbert Chapman, the manager of London's Arsenal club. He devised the influential alignment described as 3–2–2–3, or the W-M (referring to the diagrammatic pattern), deploying three defensive players supporting the goalkeeper (the top of the W), two pairs of players occupying the midfield, and three players leading the attack (the bottom of the M). See Wilson, *Inverting the Pyramid*, 42–56.

15. Wilson, *Inverting the Pyramid*, 119–121.

16. Wilson, *Inverting the Pyramid*, 218.

17. Parke H. Davis, *Football: The American Intercollegiate Game* (New York: Charles Scribner's Sons, 1911), 278.

18. S. C. Gwynne, *The Perfect Pass: American Genius and the Reinvention of Football* (New York: Scribner, 2016), 105.

19. Coaches Fred "Tex" Winter and Phil Jackson, who joined forces leading the Chicago Bulls and Los Angeles Lakers, practiced a celebrated, if controversial, approach to the triangle offense. See Nicholas Dawidoff, "The Obtuse Triangle," *New York Times*, June 23, 2015, https://www.nytimes.com/2015/06/28/sports/basketball/phil-jackson-knicks-triangle-offense-nba.html; Tex Winter, "The Triangle Offense," *FIBA Assist Magazine*, July/August 2007, 8–22, http://www.kosarkarski-trenerji.com/ftp/fiba/a27.pdf.

20. Kirk Goldsberry, *Sprawlball: A Visual Tour of the New Era of the NBA* (Boston: Houghton Mifflin Harcourt, 2019), 11.

21. During the 2017–2018 season, for example, 36 percent of three-point shots were successful (players specializing in outside shooting had a 40 percent success rate) compared to a 50 percent success rate for two-point shots. At this level of performance, the discrepancy in accuracy is offset by the higher value of a three-point shot. Goldsberry, *Sprawlball*, 207.

22. For the Bulls' 1990–1991 statistics, see https://www.basketball-reference.com/teams/CHI/1991.html. For the Warriors' 2016–2017 statistics, see https://www.basketball-reference.com/teams/GSW/2017.html.

23. Victor Mather, "How the N.B.A. 3-Point Shot Went from Gimmick to Game Changer," *New York Times*, January 21, 2016, https://www.nytimes.com/2016/01/21/sports/basketball/how-the-nba-3-point-shot-went-from-gimmick-to-game-changer.html.

24. Grant Wahl, *Masters of Modern Soccer: How the World's Best Play the Twenty-First-Century Game* (New York: Crown Archetype, 2018), 171.

25. Schonbrun, *Performance Cortex*. For mirror neurons, see 233ff.; for network models, see the discussion of the research by Emily Cross on action observation networks, 236ff. On implications for architecture, see Mallgrave, *Architecture and Embodiment*, 139.

26. Quoted in Schonbrun, *Performance Cortex*, 263. See Jia Han et al., "Assessing Proprioception: A Critical Review of Methods," *Journal of Sport and Health Science* 5, no. 1 (2016), https://doi.org/10.1016/j.jshs.2014.10.004.

27. Schonbrun, *Performance Cortex*, 272ff. See also Tohoku University, "Eyes in the Back of the Head," Science Daily, May 10, 2018, https://www.sciencedaily.com/releases/2018/05/180510115056.htm.

28. Wahl, *Masters of Modern Soccer*, 84.

29. Csikszentmihalyi, *Flow*, 39.

30. Onaje X. O. Woodbine, *Black Gods of the Asphalt: Religion, Hip-Hop, and Street Basketball* (New York: Columbia University Press,

2016), 11.

31. For an introduction and literature review, see Irena Martínková, "Phenomenology and Sport," in *Routledge Handbook of the Philosophy of Sport*, ed. Mike McNamee and William J. Morgan (London and New York: Routledge, 2015).

32. Maurice Merleau-Ponty, *The Structure of Behavior*, trans. Alden L. Fisher (Boston: Beacon Press, 1963), 168–169. For analysis of Merleau-Ponty's phenomenology applied specifically to soccer, see John Hughson and Simon Inglis, "Inside the Beautiful Game: Towards a Merleau-Pontian Phenomenology of Soccer Play," *Journal of the Philosophy of Sport* 29, no. 1 (2002): 1–15.

33. Kenneth Aggerholm, Ejgil Jespersen, and Lars Tore Ronglan, "Falling for the Feint: An Existential Investigation of a Creative Performance in High-level Football," *Sport, Ethics and Philosophy* 5, no. 3 (October 11, 2011), https://doi.org/10.1080/17511321.2011.602589.

34. Woodbine, *Black Gods of the Asphalt*, 160.

35. The philosopher David Best distinguishes "purposive" sports, in which the aesthetic is relatively unimportant, from "aesthetic" sports, in which the aim by definition includes the aesthetic. Best, *Philosophy and Human Movement*, 104–105. See also Holt, *Kinetic Beauty*, 76–86.

36. For analytic frameworks, see Gumbrecht, *In Praise of Athletic Beauty*; Holt, *Kinetic Beauty*. For extended discussion of aesthetics in soccer, including its spatial implications, see Stephen D. Mumford, *Football: The Philosophy behind the Game* (Cambridge: Polity Press, 2019).

37. Yuriko Saito, "Aesthetics of the Everyday," Stanford Encyclopedia of Philosophy Archive, September 30, 2015, https://plato.stanford.edu/archives/win2015/entries/aesthetics-of-everyday/.

38. Kalle Puolakka, "Dewey and Everyday Aesthetics—A New Look," *Contemporary Aesthetics*, no. 12 (2014), https://digitalcommons.risd.edu/liberalarts_contempaesthetics/vol12/iss1/18/.

39. John Dewey, *Art as Experience* (New York: Berkley Publishing Group, 2005), 22.

40. Dewey, *Art as Experience*, 38. Emphasis in original.

41. Tim L. Elcombe, "Philosophers Can't Jump: Reflections on Living Time and Space in Basketball," in *Basketball and Philosophy: Thinking outside the Paint*, ed. Jerry L. Walls and Gregory Bassham (Lexington: University Press of Kentucky, 2007). Elcombe draws on Dewey's book *Experience and Nature* (1938).

42. Elcombe, "Philosophers Can't Jump," 217.

43. I thank the architect and longtime Masters swimmer Stefani Danes for her observations. For a study of swim training from the perspective of sociological phenomenology, see Gareth McNarry, Jacquelyn Allen-Collinson, and Adam B. Evans, "'Doing' Competitive Swimming: Exploring the Skilled Practices of the Competitive Swimming Lifeworld," *International Review for the Sociology of Sport* 56,

no. 1 (2021): 3–19, https://doi.org/10.1177/1012690219894939. For the application of sports performance analytics to proprioception, see Jenny Vrentas, "Why Some Olympic Swimmers Think about Math in the Pool," *New York Times*, July 29, 2024, https://www.nytimes.com/2024/07/29/world/olympics/olympics-swimming-data-analytics.html.

44. Berleant, *Art and Engagement*, 89.

45. Berleant, *Art and Engagement*, 91.

46. Berleant, *Art and Engagement*, 97. See also Barbara Montero, "Proprioception as an Aesthetic Sense," *Journal of Aesthetics and Art Criticism* 64, no. 2 (Spring 2006). For discussion of implications of her study for architecture, see Mallgrave, *Architecture and Embodiment*, 148–151.

47. Pallasmaa, *Eyes of the Skin*, 99.

48. Michael Novak, *The Joy of Sports: End Zones, Bases, Baskets, Balls, and the Consecration of the American Spirit* (Lanham, MD: Hamilton Press, 1967), 123.

49. Novak, *Joy of Sports*, 125–126.

50. Gumbrecht, *In Praise of Athletic Beauty*, 205. See also Hans Ulrich Gumbrecht, *Crowds: The Stadium as a Ritual of Intensity*, trans. Emily Goodling (Stanford, CA: Stanford University Press, 2021); Mumford, *Watching Sport*. Mumford situates partisans and purists at the opposing poles of spectatorship.

51. Friedrich Nietzsche, *The Birth of Tragedy*, trans. Douglas Smith (Oxford, UK: Oxford University Press, 2000).

52. Angell, *Summer Game*, 302–303.

53. Alan Blinder and David Waldstein, "The Braves, the Cardinals and an Infamous Infield Fly: An Oral History," *New York Times*, October 3, 2019, https://www.nytimes.com/2019/10/03/sports/braves-cardinals-baseball-playoff.html.

54. For a summary, see Holt, *Kinetic Beauty*, 19–22.

55. Gumbrecht, *In Praise of Athletic Beauty*, 168–169.

56. Christopher Cordner, "The Meaning of Graceful Movement," *Journal of the Philosophy of Sport* 30, no. 2 (2003): 137. Emphasis in original.

57. Cordner, "Meaning of Graceful Movement," 142. Emphasis in original.

58. David Michael Levin, "Balanchine's Formalism," *Salmagundi*, no. 33/34 (Spring–Summer 1976): 228.

59. Woodbine, *Black Gods of the Asphalt*, 162–163.

60. Borden, *Skateboarding, Space and the City*, 91.

61. Borden, *Skateboarding, Space and the City*, 100.

62. Borden, *Skateboarding, Space and the City*, 105. Emphasis in original.

63. Alongside Borden's work on skateboarding, there are numerous studies examining the challenges to power and social conventions

in parkour; see Jimena Ortuzar, "Parkour or l'art du déplacement: A Kinetic Urban Utopia," *TDR: The Drama Review* 53, no. 3 (2009): 54–66.

64. Signe Højbjerre Larsen, "What Can the Parkour Craftsmen Tell Us about Bodily Expertise and Skilled Movement?," *Sport, Ethics and Philosophy* 10, no. 3 (2016): 301, https://doi.org/10.1080/17511321.2016.1217919.

## CHAPTER 4. SPORTS, SPACE, AND CULTURE

1. Hermann Hertzberger, *Lessons for Students in Architecture*, 4th ed. (Rotterdam: 010 Publishers, 2013), 149. Quoted in Winner, *Brilliant Orange*, 29.

2. Winner, *Brilliant Orange*, 46–47.

3. Winner, *Brilliant Orange*, 47.

4. For an overview of place theory, see Tim Cresswell, *Place: A Short Introduction* (Oxford, UK: Blackwell, 2004). For the application of the concept to sports, see Bale, *Sports Geography*, 14–35.

5. Novak, *Joy of Sports*, 126.

6. William W. Kelly, "Kōshien Stadium: Performing National Virtues and Regional Rivalries in a 'Theatre of Sport,'" *Sport in Society* 14, no. 4 (2011): 482–494, https://doi.org/10.1080/17430437.2011.565926.

7. Neville Gabie, "Goalposts: A Neville Gabie Project," http://www.nevillegabiegoalposts.co.uk/; Van der Meer, "European Fields"; Jeff Wilson, *Home Field: Texas High School Football Stadiums from Alice to Zephyr* (Austin: University of Texas Press, 2010).

8. Richard J. Puerzer, "The Annual Forbes Field Celebration: Pirates Fans Relive Mazeroski's Moment," in *The National Pastime: Steel City Stories (Pittsburgh, 2018)*, ed. Cecilia M. Tan (Lincoln, NE: Society for American Baseball Research and the University of Nebraska Press, 2018).

9. Jason Wood and Neville Gabie, "The Football Ground and Visual Culture: Recapturing Place, Memory and Meaning at Ayresome Park," *International Journal of the History of Sport* 28, no. 8–9 (2011), https://doi.org/10.1080/09523367.2011.567771.

10. See, for example, the English-language guide published by the Japan Sumo Association, Nihon Sumo Kyokai, *The Sumo*, (Tokyo: 2014).

11. Wolfram Manzenreiter, "Cracks in the Moral Economy of Sumo: Beasts of Burden, Sports Heroes, National Icons and Living Gods in Disgrace," *International Journal of the History of Sport* 31, no. 4 (2014): 462, https://doi.org/10.1080/09523367.2013.869213.

12. For summaries of sumo's history, see Allen Guttmann and Lee Thompson, *Japanese Sports: A History* (Honolulu: University of Hawai'i Press, 2001), 13–26, 108–116; Manzenreiter, "Cracks in the Moral Economy of Sumo"; Roderic Kenji Tierney, "Wrestling with Tradition: Sumo, National Identity and Trans/National Popular Culture"

(PhD diss., University of California, Berkeley, 2002).

13. Tierney, "Wrestling with Tradition," 43.

14. Manzenreiter, "Cracks in the Moral Economy of Sumo," 464; Tierney, "Wrestling with Tradition," 148–151.

15. Paul Rouse, *The Hurlers: The First All-Ireland Championship and the Making of Modern Hurling* (Dublin: Penguin Ireland, 2018).

16. Mark Doidge, "*Il Calcio* as a Source of Local and Social Identity in Italy," in *Identity Discourses and Communities in International Events, Festivals and Spectacles*, ed. Udo Merkel (Houndmills, UK: Palgrave Macmillan, 2015), 41.

17. Bale, *Landscapes of Modern Sport*, 153. Also see John Bale, "Cricket," in *The Theater of Sport*, ed. Karl B. Raitz (Baltimore: Johns Hopkins University Press, 1995).

18. Bale, *Sports Geography*, 159–161.

19. Goldberger, *Ballpark*, 38.

20. Bradd Shore, *Culture in Mind: Cognition, Culture, and the Problem of Meaning* (New York: Oxford University Press, 1996), chapter 3.

21. The cultural associations of baseball are not universal. Baseball in Japan, where it has been played since the 1870s, is celebrated more as the expression of collective values of teamwork than with an emphasis on individual achievement, as in the American game. See Robert Whiting, *You Gotta Have Wa*, 2nd rev. ed. (New York: Vintage Books, 2009); William W. Kelly, "Samurai Baseball: The Vicissitudes of a National Sporting Style," *International Journal of the History of Sport* 26, no. 3 (2009): 429–441, https://doi.org/10.1080/09523360802602299; Christopher T. Keaveney, *Contesting the Myths of Samurai Baseball: Cultural Representations of Japan's National Pastime* (Hong Kong: Hong Kong University Press, 2018).

22. Goldberger, *Ballpark*, 15–16.

23. W. P. Kinsella, *Shoeless Joe* (Boston: Houghton Mifflin, 1982), 3.

24. Leslie Heaphy, "Black Women Playing Baseball: An Introduction," *Baseball Research Journal* (Spring 2022), Society for American Baseball Research, https://sabr.org/journal/article/black-women-playing-baseball-an-introduction/; Jameson Cohen, "The All-American Girls Professional Baseball League: Frontiers and Femininity in America's Favorite Pastime," *Baseball Research Journal* (Spring 2022), Society for American Baseball Research, https://sabr.org/journal/article/the-all-american-girls-professional-baseball-league-frontiers-and-femininity-in-americas-favorite-pastime/.

25. Morris, *Game of Inches*, 498–499.

26. Jean-Marie Brohm, *Sport, a Prison of Measured Time: Essays*, trans. Ian Fraser (London: Ink Links Ltd., 1978).

27. For women's amateur softball, see Susan Birrell and Diana M. Richter, "Is a Diamond Forever? Feminist Transformations of Sport," *Women's Studies International Forum* 10, no. 4 (1987): 395–409, https://doi.org/10.1016/0277-5395(87)90057-4.

28. Donald M. Fisher, *Lacrosse: A History of the Game* (Baltimore: The Johns Hopkins University Press, 2002), 24; Allan Downey, *The Creator's Game: Lacrosse, Identity, and Indigenous Nationhood* (Vancouver: University of British Columbia Press, 2018), 44.

29. Beers, *Lacrosse*, 55.

30. Beers, *Lacrosse*, 32.

31. Beers, *Lacrosse*, 54.

32. Patrick F. McDevitt, *May the Best Man Win: Sport, Masculinity, and Nationalism in Great Britain and the Empire, 1880–1935* (New York: Palgrave Macmillan, 2004).

33. Beers, *Lacrosse*, xv.

34. Downey, *Creator's Game*, 43.

35. Downey, *Creator's Game*, 254–256.

36. Andrew Heisel, "The Plot to Kill the Slam Dunk," *Vice*, February 12, 2015, https://www.vice.com/en/article/xyj9gk/the-plot-to-kill-the-slam-dunk.

37. Yago Colás, *Ball Don't Lie! Myth, Genealogy, and Invention in the Culture of Basketball* (Philadelphia: Temple University Press, 2016).

38. Artist's statement shared by Johan Ferner Ström with the author, March 24, 2020. For images of his installations, see www.johanstrom.com.

39. Lieven Ameel and Sirpa Tani, "Everyday Aesthetics in Action: Parkour Eyes and the Beauty of Concrete Walls," *Emotion, Space and Society* 5, no. 3 (2012): 166.

40. Borden, *Skateboarding, Space and the City*, 192.

41. Signe Højbjerre Larsen, "Parkour: Playing the Modern, Accelerated City," *Journal of the Philosophy of Sport* 48, no. 1 (March 2021): 34. Emphasis in original.

42. Woodbine, *Black Gods of the Asphalt*, 16–17.

43. Woodbine, *Black Gods of the Asphalt*, 12–13.

EPILOGUE. BIG AIR

1. Sherman R. Poppen, Surf-Type Snow Ski, US Patent 3,378,274, filed March 17, 1966.

2. For a vivid account of the early days of competitive snowboarding, see Todd Richards and Eric Blehm, *P3: Pipes, Parks, and Powder* (New York: ReganBooks, 2003).

3. For a concise summary of the tradeoffs of snowboarding's rise as an Olympic sport, see Holly Thorpe and Belinda Wheaton, "How Snowboarding Became a Marquee Event at the Winter Olympics—But Lost Some of Its Cool Factor in the Process," The Conversation, February 1, 2022, https://theconversation.com/how-snowboarding-became-a-marquee-event-at-the-winter-olympics-but-lost-some-of-its-cool-factor-in-the-process-175053.

4. Lee Crane, "A Complete History of the Snowboard Halfpipe,"

*Snowboarder*, November 30, 1996, https://www.snowboarder.com/transworld-snowboarding-archive/snowboarding-photos/a-complete-history-of-the-snowboard-halfpipe/.

5. Crane, "Complete History of the Snowboard Halfpipe."

6. Rain Noe, "How Snowboard Halfpipes Are Made," Core77, February 13, 2018, https://www.core77.com/posts/73316/How-Snowboard-Halfpipes-are-Made.

7. "The Dragon Lives On: Pipe Dragon Inventor Doug Waugh Passes Away," *Snowboarder*, February 29, 2000, https://www.snowboarder.com/transworld-snowboarding-archive/snowboarding-photos/the-dragon-lives-on-pipe-dragon-inventor-doug-waugh-passes-away/.

8. "Halfpipe Construction: The Shape of Things to Come," *Snowboarder*, December 5, 1996, https://www.snowboarder.com/transworld-snowboarding-archive/snowboarding-how-to/halfpipe-construction-the-shape-of-things-to-come/.

9. Noe, "How Snowboard Halfpipes Are Made."

10. *Lift-off: The Story of the Superpipe*, episode 2, "Part 2, The Evolution," aired April 11, 2021, on NBC.

11. Parker Bohon, host, The Blade Dive, episode 23, "Jeremy Carpenter," July 13, 2021, 1 hr., 44 min. 16 sec., https://www.listennotes.com/top-podcasts/jeremy-carpenter/.

12. *Halfpipe Hype*, episode 1, "The Joy of Halfpipe Riding," The Olympic Channel, 2021, video, 4 min., 49 sec., https://olympics.com/en/original-series/episode/halfpipe-hype-the-joy-of-riding?uxreference=playlist.

13. Merce Cunningham, "The Impermanent Art," *7 Arts*, no. 3 (1995): 69–77, https://www.mercecunningham.org/the-work/writings/the-impermanent-art/.

14. Henri Lefebvre, *The Production of Space*, trans. Donald Nicholson-Smith (Oxford, UK: Basil Blackwell, 1991), 205–206. Borden deftly employs Lefebvre's thought to his analysis of skateboarding; see Borden, *Skateboarding, Space and the City*, 112–113. Rhythm was a key concept for John Dewey; see Dewey, *Art as Experience*.

15. Sigmund Loland, "Outline of a Phenomenology of Snowboarding," in *Philosophy, Risk and Adventure Sports*, ed. Mike McNamee (London: Routledge, 2007), 113.

16. *Lift-off: The Story of the Superpipe*, episode 3, "Part 3, A Whole New Game," aired April 11, 2021, on NBC.

17. John Branch, "Sometimes Shaun White's Troubles Start When He's 20 Feet in the Air," *New York Times*, February 8, 2022, https://www.nytimes.com/2022/02/08/sports/olympics/shaun-white-olympics-snowboard.html.

18. Andrew Keh, "Sarah Burke, Freestyle Skier, Dies from Injuries in Training," *New York Times*, January 19, 2012, https://www.nytimes.com/2012/01/20/sports/skiing/sarah-burke-canadian-freestyle-skier

-dies-from-injuries.html.

19. For discussion of possible directions for halfpipe competitions, see *Lift-off: The Story of the Superpipe,* episode 4, "Part 4, The Modern Era," aired April 11, 2021, on NBC; Bohon, "Jeremy Carpenter."

20. Krakauer and Viera, "Keeping Your Eye on the Ball."

# BIBLIOGRAPHY


Adams, Audrey. "Radio Football down the Years." BBC. January 14, 2002. https://news.bbc.co.uk/sport2/hi/football/1760579.stm.

Aggerholm, Kenneth, Ejgil Jespersen, and Lars Tore Ronglan. "Falling for the Feint: An Existential Investigation of a Creative Performance in High-Level Football." *Sport, Ethics and Philosophy* 5, no. 3 (October 11, 2011): 343–358. https://doi.org/10.1080/17511321.2011.602589.

Ameel, Lieven, and Sirpa Tani. "Everyday Aesthetics in Action: Parkour Eyes and the Beauty of Concrete Walls." *Emotion, Space and Society* 5, no. 3 (2012): 164–173.

Angell, Roger. "Distance: The Game Belongs to Bob Gibson." *New Yorker*, September 22, 1980. https://www.newyorker.com/magazine/1980/09/22/distance.

Angell, Roger. *The Summer Game*. New York: Viking Press, 1972.

Baccellieri, Emma. "What's behind MLB's Fake Crowd Noise? A Conductor with an iPad." *Sports Illustrated*, September 5, 2020. https://www.si.com/mlb/2020/09/05/baseball-fake-crowd-nosie.

Bachelard, Gaston. *The Poetics of Space*. Translated by Maria Jolas. Boston: Beacon Press, 1969.

Baerwald, Thomas J. "Basketball." In *The Theater of Sport*, edited by Karl B. Raitz, 168–207. Baltimore: Johns Hopkins University Press, 1995.

Bale, John. "Cricket." In *The Theater of Sport*, edited by Karl B. Raitz, 70–96. Baltimore: Johns Hopkins University Press, 1995.

Bale, John. *Landscapes of Modern Sport*. Leicester, UK: Leicester University Press, 1994.

Bale, John. "Space, Place and Body Culture: Yi-Fu Tuan and a Geography of Sport." *Geografiska Annaler. Series B, Human Geography* 78, no. 3 (1996): 163–171.

Bale, John. *Sports Geography*. 2nd ed. London: Routledge, 2003.

"Baseball: The Professional Arena." *Brooklyn Daily Eagle* (Brooklyn, NY). June 1, 1875, 2. https://bklyn.newspapers.com/image/50419715.

Beers, William George. *Lacrosse: The National Game of Canada*. Montreal: Dawson Brothers, 1869.

Belsky, Gary, and Neil Fine. *On the Origins of Sports: The Early History and Original Rules of Everybody's Favorite Games*. New York: Artisan, 2016.

Berleant, Arnold. *Art and Engagement*. Philadelphia: Temple University Press, 1991.

Berman, Gary. "The First Olympics on Television (It Wasn't in the U.S.)." Medium, July 22, 2021.

Best, David. *Philosophy and Human Movement*. London: George Allen & Unwin, 1978.

Birrell, Susan, and Diana M. Richter. "Is a Diamond Forever? Feminist Transformations of Sport." *Women's Studies International Forum* 10, no. 4 (1987): 395–409. https://doi.org/10.1016/0277-5395(87)90057-4.

Blinder, Alan, and David Waldstein. "The Braves, the Cardinals and an Infamous Infield Fly: An Oral History." *New York Times*, October 3, 2019.

Bloomer, Kent C., Charles W. Moore, and Robert J. Yudell. *Body, Memory, and Architecture*. New Haven, CT: Yale University Press, 1977.

Bogost, Ian. *Play Anything: The Pleasure of Limits, the Uses of Boredom, and the Secret of Games*. New York: Basic Books, 2016.

Bohon, Parker, host. The Blade Dive. Episode 23, "Jeremy Carpenter." July 13, 2021. Podcast, 1 hr., 44 min, 16 sec. https://www.listennotes.com/top-podcasts/jeremy-carpenter/.

Borden, Iain. *Skateboarding, Space and the City*. Oxford, UK: Berg, 2001.

Borden, Iain. *Skateboarding and the City: A Complete History*. London: Bloomsbury Visual Arts, 2019.

Branch, John. "Sometimes Shaun White's Troubles Start When He's 20 Feet in the Air." *New York Times*, February 8, 2022. https://www.nytimes.com/2022/02/08/sports/olympics/shaun-white-olympics-snowboard.html.

Breech, John. "NFL Gets Thrown under the Bus for Slippery Super Bowl Field Conditions That One Player Called the 'Worst' Ever." CBS Sports, February 16, 2023. https://www.cbssports.com/nfl/news/nfl-gets-thrown-under-the-bus-for-slippery-super-bowl-field-conditions-that-one-player-called-the-worst-ever/.

Brohm, Jean-Marie. *Sport, a Prison of Measured Time: Essays*. Translated by Ian Fraser. London: Ink Links Ltd., 1978.

Chadwick, Henry, ed. *Spalding's Official Base Ball Guide*. Vol. 1900. New York: American Sports Publishing Company, 1900.

Cherry, Robert Allen. *Wilt: Larger than Life*. Chicago: Triumph Books, 2004.

Cleary, Richard. "The Architecture of Sports." *Places Journal*, July 2017. https://doi.org/10.22269/170725.

Cleary, Richard. "Fields of Play: Laboratories of Spatial Invention." In *Landscapes for Sport: Histories of Exercise, Sport, and Health*, edited by Sonja Dümpelmann, 123–140. Washington, DC: Dumbarton Oaks Research Library and Collection, 2022.

Cleary, Richard. "Well Played! An Architectural View of Sports." In

*Resplendent Adventures with Britannia: Personalities, Politics and Culture in Britain*, edited by Wm. Roger Louis, 339–352. London and Austin, TX: I. B. Tauris and Harry Ransom Center, 2015.

Cohen, Jameson. "The All-American Girls Professional Baseball League: Frontiers and Femininity in America's Favorite Pastime." *Baseball Research Journal* (Spring 2022). Society for American Baseball Research. https://sabr.org/journal/article/the-all-american-girls-professional-baseball-league-frontiers-and-femininity-in-americas-favorite-pastime/.

Colás, Yago. *Ball Don't Lie! Myth, Genealogy, and Invention in the Culture of Basketball*. Philadelphia: Temple University Press, 2016.

Collins, Harry. "The Philosophy of Umpiring and the Introduction of Decision-Aid Technology." *Journal of the Philosophy of Sport* 37, no. 2 (2010): 135–146.

Cordner, Christopher. "The Meaning of Graceful Movement." *Journal of the Philosophy of Sport* 30, no. 2 (2003): 132–143.

Crane, Lee. "A Complete History of the Snowboard Halfpipe." *Snowboarder*, November 30, 1996. https://www.snowboarder.com/transworld-snowboarding-archive/snowboarding-photos/a-complete-history-of-the-snowboard-halfpipe/.

Crenshaw, Ben, and Melanie Hauser. *A Feel for the Game: To Brookline and Back*. New York: Doubleday, 2001.

Cresswell, Tim. *Place: A Short Introduction*. Oxford, UK: Blackwell, 2004.

Csikszentmihalyi, Mihaly. *Flow: The Psychology of Optimal Experience*. New York: HarperCollins, 1990.

Cunningham, Merce. "The Impermanent Art." *7 Arts*, no. 3 (1995): 69–77. https://www.mercecunningham.org/the-work/writings/the-impermanent-art/.

Dant, Tim. *Television and the Moral Imaginary: Society through the Small Screen*. Houndmills, UK: Palgrave Macmillan, 2012.

Davis, Parke H. *Football: The American Intercollegiate Game*. New York: Charles Scribner's Sons, 1911.

Dawidoff, Nicholas. "The Obtuse Triangle." *New York Times*, June 23, 2015. https://www.nytimes.com/2015/06/28/sports/basketball/phil-jackson-knicks-triangle-offense-nba.html.

Dewey, John. *Art as Experience*. New York: Berkley Publishing Group, 2005.

Doak, Tom. *The Anatomy of a Golf Course*. New York: Lyons and Burford, 1992.

Doak, Tom, James S. Scott, and Raymund M. Haddock. *The Life and Work of Dr. Alister Mackenzie*. Chelsea, MI: Sleeping Bear Press, 2001.

Doidge, Mark. "*Il Calcio* as a Source of Local and Social Identity in Italy." In *Identity Discourses and Communities in International Events, Festivals and Spectacles*, edited by Udo Merkel, 37–53. Houndmills, UK: Palgrave Macmillan, 2015.

Downey, Allan. *The Creator's Game: Lacrosse, Identity, and Indigenous Nationhood*. Vancouver: University of British Columbia Press, 2018.

"The Dragon Lives On: Pipe Dragon Inventor Doug Waugh Passes Away." *Snowboarder*, February 29, 2000. https://www.snowboarder.com/transworld-snowboarding-archive/snowboarding-photos/the-dragon-lives-on-pipe-dragon-inventor-doug-waugh-passes-away/.

Dümpelmann, Sonja. *Landscapes for Sport: Histories of Physical Exercise, Sport, and Health*. Washington, DC: Dumbarton Oaks Research Library and Collection, 2022.

Elcombe, Tim L. "Philosophers Can't Jump: Reflections on Living Time and Space in Basketball." In *Basketball and Philosophy: Thinking outside the Paint*, edited by Jerry L. Walls and Gregory Bassham, 207–219. Lexington: University Press of Kentucky, 2007.

Feinberg, Robert. "Does Moving the NBA 3-Point Line Help Good 3-Point Shooting Teams?" Harvard Sports Analysis Collective (blog), May 31, 2017. http://harvardsportsanalysis.org/2017/05/does-moving-the-nba-3-point-line-help-good-3-point-shooting-teams/.

Fernandez, Gabriel. "LOOK: Oklahoma State Displays Yellow Lines on Video Board to Distract Texas Kicker's Field Goal Attempt." CBS Sports, October 31, 2020. https://www.cbssports.com/college-football/news/look-oklahoma-state-displays-yellow-lines-on-video-board-to-distract-texas-kickers-field-goal-attempt/.

Feuer, Jane. "The Concept of Live Television: Ontology as Ideology." In *Regarding Television: Critical Approaches—an Anthology*, edited by E. Ann Kaplan, 12–21. Frederick, MD: University Publications of America, 1983.

Fisher, Donald M. *Lacrosse: A History of the Game*. Baltimore: Johns Hopkins University Press, 2002.

Flowers, Benjamin. *Beautiful Moves: Designing Stadia*. London: Lund Humphries, 2018.

Flowers, Benjamin S. *Sport and Architecture*. Milton Park, UK: Routledge, 2017.

Gabie, Neville. "Goalposts: A Neville Gabie Project." Accessed November 11, 2024. http://www.nevillegabiegoalposts.co.uk/.

Galeano, Eduardo. *Soccer in Sun and Shadow*. Translated by Mark Fried. 2nd paperback ed. London: Verso, 2003.

Gamache, Ray. *A History of Sports Highlights: Replayed Plays from Edison to ESPN*. Jefferson, NC: McFarland and Company, 2010.

Garber, Greg. "Jumbotron: The Big Picture." ESPN. Accessed November 11, 2024. http://www.espn.com/nfl/feature/featureVideo?page=jumbotron.

Ghisleni, Camilla. "What Is Hedonistic Sustainability in Architecture?" ArchDaily, September 4, 2023. https://www.archdaily.com/1006443/what-is-hedonistic-sustainability-in-architecture.

Goldberger, Paul. *Ballpark: Baseball in the American City*. New York: Alfred A. Knopf, 2019.

Goldblatt, David. *The Ball Is Round: A Global History of Football*. New York: Riverhead Books, 2008.

Goldsberry, Kirk. *Sprawlball: A Visual Tour of the New Era of the NBA*. Boston: Houghton Mifflin Harcourt, 2019.

Greene, Nick. *How to Watch Basketball like a Genius: What Game Designers, Economists, Ballet Choreographers, and Theoretical Physicists Reveal about the Greatest Game on Earth*. New York: Abrams Press, 2021.

Greene, Nick. "Is CBS Piping Fake Birds into Its Masters Coverage?" Slate, April 12, 2019. https://slate.com/culture/2019/04/masters-cbs-coverage-birds-real-fake.html.

Gulick, Luther, ed. *Official Basket Ball Rules as Adopted by the Young Men's Christian Association Athletic League of North America*. Spalding's Athletic Library: Official Basket Ball Guide, Season 1896–1897. New York: American Sports Publishing Company, 1896.

Gumbrecht, Hans Ulrich. *Crowds: The Stadium as a Ritual of Intensity*. Translated by Emily Goodling. Stanford, CA: Stanford University Press, 2021.

Gumbrecht, Hans Ulrich. *In Praise of Athletic Beauty*. Cambridge, MA: Harvard University Press, 2006.

Guttmann, Allen, and Lee Thompson. *Japanese Sports: A History*. Honolulu: University of Hawai'i Press, 2001.

Gwynne, S. C. *The Perfect Pass: American Genius and the Reinvention of Football*. New York: Scribner, 2016.

"Halfpipe Construction: The Shape of Things to Come." *Snowboarder*, December 5, 1996. https://www.snowboarder.com/transworld-snowboarding-archive/snowboarding-how-to/halfpipe-construction-the-shape-of-things-to-come/.

*Halfpipe Hype*. Episode 1, "The Joy of Halfpipe Riding." The Olympic Channel, 2021. Video, 4 min., 49 sec. https://olympics.com/en/original-series/episode/halfpipe-hype-the-joy-of-riding?uxreference=playlist.

Han, Jia, Gordon Waddington, Roger Adams, Judith Anson, and Yu Liu. "Assessing Proprioception: A Critical Review of Methods." *Journal of Sport and Health Science* 5, no. 1 (2016): 80–90. https://doi.org/10.1016/j.jshs.2014.10.004.

Hanson, Christopher. "The Instant Replay: Time and Time Again." *Spectator* [USC] 28, no. 2 (Fall 2008): 51–60.

Heaphy, Leslie. "Black Women Playing Baseball: An Introduction." *Baseball Research Journal* (Spring 2022). Society for American Baseball Research. https://sabr.org/journal/article/black-women-playing-baseball-an-introduction/.

Heisel, Andrew. "The Plot to Kill the Slam Dunk." *Vice*, February 12, 2015. https://www.vice.com/en/article/xyj9gk/the-plot-to-kill-the-slam-dunk.

Helfand, Zach. "Kill the Umpire." *New Yorker*, August 30, 2021, 24–28.

Helphand, Kenneth I. "Learning from Linksland." *Landscape Journal* 14, no. 1 (Spring 1995): 74–86.

Herbert, James. "NBA to Use Interactive LED Glass Court at 2024 All-Star Weekend: Here's How 'Huge Television Screen' Will Work." CBS Sports. February 5, 2024. https://www.cbssports.com/nba/news/nba-to-use-interactive-led-glass-court-at-2024-all-star-weekend-heres-how-huge-television-screen-will-work/.

Hertzberger, Hermann. *Lessons for Students in Architecture*. 4th ed. Rotterdam: 010 Publishers, 2013.

Hines, James R. *Figure Skating: A History*. Urbana: University of Illinois Press and World Figure Skating Museum and Hall of Fame, 2006.

Hintz, Eric S. "The Invention of Instant Replay." Lemelson Center for the Study of Invention and Innovation, Smithsonian Institution. January 20, 2022. https://invention.si.edu/invention-instant-replay.

Holt, Jason. *Kinetic Beauty: The Philosophical Aesthetics of Sport*. Abingdon, UK: Routledge, 2020.

Hughson, John, and Simon Inglis. "Inside the Beautiful Game: Towards a Merleau-Pontian Phenomenology of Soccer Play." *Journal of the Philosophy of Sport* 29, no. 1 (2002): 1–15.

Huizinga, Johan. *Homo Ludens: A Study of the Play-Element in Culture*. Translated by R. F. C. Hull. London: Routledge & Kegan Paul, 1949.

Jackson, Steven J., and Brendan Hokowhitu. "Sport, Tribes, and Technology: The New Zealand All Blacks Haka and the Politics of Identity." *Journal of Sport and Social Issues* 26, no. 2 (2002): 125–139.

Jones, Robert Trent, Jr. *Golf by Design: How to Lower Your Score by Reading the Features of a Course*. Boston: Little, Brown and Company, 1993.

Kahn, Louis. "Architecture Is the Thoughtful Making of Spaces." *Perspecta*, no. 4 (1957): 2–3.

Keaveney, Christopher T. *Contesting the Myths of Samurai Baseball: Cultural Representations of Japan's National Pastime*. Hong Kong: Hong Kong University Press, 2018.

Keh, Andrew. "Sarah Burke, Freestyle Skier, Dies from Injuries in Training." *New York Times*, January 19, 2012. https://www.nytimes.com/2012/01/20/sports/skiing/sarah-burke-canadian-freestyle-skier-dies-from-injuries.html.

Keh, Andrew. "We Hope Your Cheers for This Article Are for Real." *New York Times*, June 17, 2020. https://www.nytimes.com/2020/06/16/sports/coronavirus-stadium-fans-crowd-noise.html.

Kelly, William W. "Kōshien Stadium: Performing National Virtues and Regional Rivalries in a 'Theatre of Sport.'" *Sport in Society* 14, no. 4 (2011): 482–494. https://doi.org/10.1080/17430437.2011.565926.

Kelly, William W. "Samurai Baseball: The Vicissitudes of a National Sporting Style." *International Journal of the History of Sport* 26, no. 3 (2009): 429–441. https://doi.org/10.1080/09523360802602299.

Kerschbaumer, Ken. "World Series 2023: Drones Are Set to Fly for Fox Sports' Coverage." *SVG News*, October 27, 2023. https://www

.sportsvideo.org/2023/10/27/drones-set-to-fly-for-fox-sports-world-series-coverage/.

Kinsella, W. P. *Shoeless Joe*. Boston: Houghton Mifflin, 1982.

Knausgaard, Karl Ove. *Autumn*. New York: Penguin, 2017.

Krakauer, John, and Patrick Vieira. "Keeping Your Eye on the Ball." New York City Football Club, April 2017. SoundCloud audio. https://soundcloud.com/nycfc/patrick-vieira-john-krakauer-keeping-your-eye-on-the-ball.

Kretchmar, R. Scott. "Game Flaws." *Journal of the Philosophy of Sport* 32, no. 1 (2005): 36–48.

Kurkowska-Budzan, Marta. "Wild Stadia: Vernacular Sport Spaces in the Polish Countryside during the Socialist Era." In *Landscapes for Sport: Histories of Physical Exercise, Sport, and Health*, edited by Sonja Dümpelmann, 141–159. Washington, DC: Dumbarton Oaks, 2022.

Lang, Eric. "Analyzing the Strike Zone as a Three-Dimensional Volume." Hardball Times, September 14, 2015. https://tht.fangraphs.com/analyzing-the-strike-zone-as-a-three-dimensional-volume/.

Larsen, Signe Højbjerre. "Parkour: Playing the Modern, Accelerated City." *Journal of the Philosophy of Sport* 48, no. 1 (March 2021): 26–44.

Larsen, Signe Højbjerre. "What Can the Parkour Craftsmen Tell Us about Bodily Expertise and Skilled Movement?" *Sport, Ethics and Philosophy* 10, no. 3 (2016): 295–309. https://doi.org/10.1080/17511321.2016.1217919.

Le Corbusier. *The City of To-morrow and Its Planning*. Translated by Frederick Etchells. New York: Payson & Clarke, 1929.

Lefebvre, Henri. *The Production of Space*. Translated by Donald Nicholson-Smith. Oxford, UK: Basil Blackwell, 1991.

Levin, David Michael. "Balanchine's Formalism." *Salmagundi*, no. 33/34 (Spring–Summer 1976): 216–236.

*Lift-off: The Story of the Superpipe*, episode 2, "Part 2, The Evolution." Aired April 11, 2021, on NBC.

*Lift-off: The Story of the Superpipe*, episode 3, "Part 3, A Whole New Game." Aired April 11, 2021, on NBC.

*Lift-off: The Story of the Superpipe*, episode 4, "Part 4, The Modern Era." Aired April 11, 2021, on NBC.

Lisle, Benjamin D. *Modern Coliseum: Stadiums and American Culture*. Philadelphia: University of Pennsylvania Press, 2017.

Loland, Sigmund. "Outline of a Phenomenology of Snowboarding." In *Philosophy, Risk and Adventure Sports*, edited by Mike McNamee, 106–117. London: Routledge, 2007.

MacKenzie, Alister. "Common Sense of Camouflage Defense." *The Military Engineer* 26, no. 145 (January–February 1934): 42–47.

MacKenzie, Alister. "Entrenchment and Camouflage." *Professional Memoires, Corps of Engineers, United States Army, and Engineer Department at Large* 9, no. 47 (September–October 1917): 547–638.

MacKenzie, Alister. *The Spirit of St. Andrews*. Chelsea, MI: Sleeping Bear Press, 1995.

Major League Baseball. *Official Baseball Rules*. New York: Office of the Commisioner of Baseball, 2021.

Mallgrave, Harry Francis. *Architecture and Embodiment: The Implications of the New Sciences and Humanities for Design*. London: Routledge, 2013.

Manzenreiter, Wolfram. "Cracks in the Moral Economy of Sumo: Beasts of Burden, Sports Heroes, National Icons and Living Gods in Disgrace." *International Journal of the History of Sport* 31, no. 4 (2014): 459–473. https://doi.org/10.1080/09523367.2013.869213.

Martínková, Irena. "Phenomenology and Sport." In *Routledge Handbook of the Philosophy of Sport*, edited by Mike McNamee and William J. Morgan, 178–206. London: Routledge, 2015.

Mather, Victor. "How the N.B.A. 3-Point Shot Went from Gimmick to Game Changer." *New York Times*, January 21, 2016. https://www.nytimes.com/2016/01/21/sports/basketball/how-the-nba-3-point-shot-went-from-gimmick-to-game-changer.html.

McAllister, Mike. "Pete Dye: The Genius Who Loathed Plans." PGA Tour, March 8, 2020. https://www.pgatour.com/long-form/2020/03/08/pete-dye-genius-course-design-tpc-sawgrass-the-players-championship.html.

McDevitt, Patrick F. *May the Best Man Win: Sport, Masculinity, and Nationalism in Great Britain and the Empire, 1880–1935*. New York: Palgrave Macmillan, 2004.

McNarry, Gareth, Jacquelyn Allen-Collinson, and Adam B. Evans. "'Doing' Competitive Swimming: Exploring the Skilled Practices of the Competitive Swimming Lifeworld." *International Review for the Sociology of Sport* 56, no. 1 (2021): 3–19. https://doi.org/10.1177/1012690219894939.

Mercer, Bill. *Play-by-Play: Tales from a Sportscasting Insider*. New York: First Taylor Trade Publishing, 2007.

Merleau-Ponty, Maurice. *The Structure of Behavior*. Translated by Alden L. Fisher. Boston: Beacon Press, 1963.

Miah, Andy. *Sport 2.0: Transforming Sports for a Digital World*. Cambridge, MA: MIT Press, 2017.

MLB. "WS1960 Gm7: Mazeroski Hits a Walk-Off Homer in Game 7." YouTube video. November 1, 2016. https://www.youtube.com/watch?v=A-OCXYjVL4U.

MLB Vault. "1952 World Series, Game 7: Yankees @ Dodgers." YouTube video. September 16, 2010. https://www.youtube.com/watch?v=hqZnPQnxO9U&t=1428s.

Monier-Williams, Montagu S., Winter Randell Pidgeon, and Arthur Dryden. *Figure Skating Simple and Combined; Being an Enlarged Edition of "Combined Figure-Skating" Arranged as a Complete Text-Book of the Art of Skating as Practised in the Leading Skating Clubs of Great Britain*. London: Horace Cox, 1892.

Montero, Barbara. "Proprioception as an Aesthetic Sense." *Journal of Aesthetics and Art Criticism* 64, no. 2 (Spring 2006): 231–242.

Morris, Peter. *A Game of Inches: The Stories behind the Innovations That Shaped Baseball.* 2nd rev. ed. Chicago: Ivan R. Dee, 2010.

Mullen, Lawrence. "Joe Aceti on Sports Television Directing." University of Nevada, Las Vegas. http://lmullen.faculty.unlv.edu/vita.2/aceti.bio.htm.

Mumford, Stephen D. *Football: The Philosophy behind the Game.* Cambridge: Polity Press, 2019.

Mumford, Stephen D. *Watching Sport: Aesthetics, Ethics and Emotion.* Ethics and Sport. Hoboken: Taylor & Francis, 2011.

Murray, Scott. "How Arsenal Blazed TV Trail, Jostling for Airtime with Cartoons and Smut." *Guardian*, September 16, 2015. https://www.theguardian.com/football/tvandradioblog/2015/sep/16/how-arsenal-blazed-tv-trail-jostling-for-airtime-with-cartoons-and-smut.

Naismith, James. "Basketball: Its Origin and Development." In *Basketball: Great Writing About America's Game*, edited by Alexander Wolff, 1–10. New York: Library of America, 2018.

Nietzsche, Friedrich. *The Birth of Tragedy*. Translated by Douglas Smith. Oxford, UK: Oxford University Press, 2000.

Nihon Sumo Kyokai (Japan Sumo Association). *The Sumo*. Tokyo, 2014.

Noe, Rain. "How Snowboard Halfpipes Are Made." Core77, February 13, 2018. https://www.core77.com/posts/73316/How-Snowboard-Halfpipes-are-Made.

Novak, Michael. *The Joy of Sports: End Zones, Bases, Baskets, Balls, and the Consecration of the American Spirit*. Lanham, MD: Hamilton Press, 1967.

Oriard, Michael. "Sports and Space." *Landscape* 21, no. 1 (1976): 32–40.

Ortuzar, Jimena. "Parkour or l'art du déplacement: A Kinetic Urban Utopia." *TDR: The Drama Review* 53, no. 3 (2009): 54–66.

Pallasmaa, Juhani. *The Eyes of the Skin: Architecture and the Senses.* Chichester, UK: John Wiley & Sons, 2005.

Patterson, Ted. *The Golden Voices of Baseball.* Champaign, IL: Sports Publishing, 2002.

Pennington, Bill, and Karen Crouse. "Attention, Second-Guessers: Golf Takes Calls (and Texts)." *New York Times*, April 13, 2013. https://www.nytimes.com/2013/04/14/sports/golf/television-viewers-flag-rule-violations-as-golf-officials-take-note.html.

Peterson, Robert W. "When the Court Was a Cage." *Sports Illustrated*, November 11, 1991, 38–40. https://vault.si.com/vault/1991/11/11/when-the-court-was-a-cage-in-the-early-days-of-pro-basketball-the-players-were-segregated-from-the-fans.

Poppen, Sherman R. Surf-Type Snow Ski. US Patent 3,378,274, filed March 17, 1966, and issued April 16, 1968.

"Pro Squash Is Taking Its Court on the Road." *New York Times*, November 9, 1984. https://www.nytimes.com/1984/11/09/sports/pro-squash-is-taking-its-court-on-the-road.html.

Puerzer, Richard J. "The Annual Forbes Field Celebration: Pirates

Fans Relive Mazeroski's Moment." In *The National Pastime: Steel City Stories (Pittsburgh, 2018)*, edited by Cecilia M. Tan. Lincoln, NE: Society for American Baseball Research and the University of Nebraska Press, 2018.

Puolakka, Kalle. "Dewey and Everyday Aesthetics—A New Look." *Contemporary Aesthetics*, no. 12 (2014). https://digitalcommons.risd.edu/liberalarts contempaesthetics/vol12/iss1/18/.

Quirmbach, Chuck. "Thousands of Recorded Voices Will Cheer Milwaukee Brewers at Miller Park." WUWM 89.7, July 24, 2020. https://www.wuwm.com/post/thousands-recorded-voices-will-cheer-milwaukee-brewers-miller-park#stream/0.

Raitz, Karl B., ed. *The Theater of Sport*. Baltimore: John Hopkins University Press, 1995.

Richards, Todd, and Eric Blehm. *P3: Pipes, Parks, and Powder*. New York: ReganBooks, 2003.

Rosen, Jody. "Behind the Scenes of the Most Spectacular Show on TV." *New York Times*, December 2, 2023. https://www.nytimes.com/2023/12/02/magazine/sunday-night-football.html.

Rouse, Paul. *The Hurlers: The First All-Ireland Championship and the Making of Modern Hurling*. Dublin: Penguin Ireland, 2018.

Saito, Yuriko. "Aesthetics of the Everyday." Stanford Encyclopedia of Philosophy Archive, September 30, 2015. https://plato.stanford.edu/archives/win2015/entries/aesthetics-of-everyday/.

Salen Tekinbaş, Katie, and Eric Zimmerman. *Rules of Play: Game Design Fundamentals*. Cambridge, MA: MIT Press, 2003.

"Satchel Paige Quotes." Baseball Almanac. Accessed July 31, 2023. https://www.baseball-almanac.com/quotes/quopaig.shtml.

Schonbrun, Zach. *The Performance Cortex: How Neuroscience Is Redefining Athletic Genius*. New York: Dutton, 2018.

Schwartz, John. "Baseball: The Counterclockwise Sport." *Baseball Research Journal* (1978): 69–72. Society for American Baseball Research. https://sabr.org/journal/article/baseball-the-counterclockwise-sport/.

Schwarz, Alan. "Stoking Excitement, Arenas Pump up the Volume." *New York Times*, June 6, 2011. https://www.nytimes.com/2011/06/07/sports/basketball/stoking-fans-excitement-arenas-pump-up-the-volume.html.

Scott, Geoffrey. *The Architecture of Humanism; A Study in the History of Taste*. London: Constable and Company, 1914.

Shieber, Tom. "The Evolution of the Baseball Diamond: Perfection Came Slowly." *Baseball Research Journal* 23 (1994): 3–13. Society for American Baseball Research. https://sabr.org/journal/article/the-evolution-of-the-baseball-diamond-perfection-came-slowly/.

Shore, Bradd. *Culture in Mind: Cognition, Culture, and the Problem of Meaning*. New York: Oxford University Press, 1996.

Shubert, Howard. *Architecture on Ice: A History of the Hockey Arena*. Montreal: McGill-Queen's University Press, 2016.

Silverman, Jonathan, ed. *Astros and Asterisks: Houston's Sign-Stealing Scandal Explained*. Austin: University of Texas Press, 2023.

Stern, Jacob. "A Fake Yellow Line Changed Football Forever." *Atlantic*, February 8, 2024. https://www.theatlantic.com/technology/archive/2024/02/football-virtual-yellow-line-augmented-reality/677384/.

Stevenson, Seth. "The Man Who Saved Tennis." Slate, November 6, 2012. https://slate.com/culture/2012/11/hawk-eye-saved-tennis-from-bad-line-calls-paul-hawkins-invention-designed-for-cricket-has-moved-to-other-sports.html.

Strozek, Przemyslaw. "Footballers in Avant-Garde Art and Socialist Realism before World War II." In *Handbuch der Sportgeschicte Osteuropas*, edited by Anke Hilbrenner, Ekaterina Emeliantseva, Christian Koller, Manfred Zeiler, and Stefan Zwicker. Bonn: Universität Bonn, 2015.

Suits, Bernard. "The Elements of Sport." In *The Philosophy of Sport: A Collection of Original Essays*, edited by Robert G. Osterhoudt, 48–64. Springfield, IL: Thomas, 1973.

Tamte, Roger R. *Walter Camp and the Creation of American Football*. Urbana: University of Illinois Press, 2018.

Tharp, Twyla. *Dance Is a Man's Sport, Too*. Performed on *Omnibus*, ABC Television. Twyla Tharp Dance Foundation, New York, 1980. https://www.twylatharp.org/works/dance-mans-sport-too.

Thomas, Mike. "The Sodfather." *Smithsonian Magazine*, April 2008. https://www.smithsonianmag.com/arts-culture/the-sodfather-31895138/.

Thorn, John. "The Game That Got Away." *Our Game*, MLB.com/BLOGS, July 3, 2012. https://ourgame.mlblogs.com/the-game-that-got-away-a385699cd936.

Thorn, John. "The New York Clipper and Sporting Weeklies of Its Time." *Our Game*, MLB.com/BLOGS, February 20, 2017. https://ourgame.mlblogs.com/the-new-york-clipper-and-sporting-weeklies-of-its-time-b343de7f474f.

Thorpe, Holly, and Belinda Wheaton. "How Snowboarding Became a Marquee Event at the Winter Olympics—But Lost Some of Its Cool Factor in the Process." The Conversation, February 1, 2022. https://theconversation.com/how-snowboarding-became-a-marquee-event-at-the-winter-olympics-but-lost-some-of-its-cool-factor-in-the-process-175053.

Tierney, Roderic Kenji. "Wrestling with Tradition: Sumo, National Identity and Trans/National Popular Culture." PhD diss., University of California, Berkeley, 2002.

Tohoku University. "Eyes in the Back of the Head." Science Daily, May 10, 2018. https://www.sciencedaily.com/releases/2018/05/180510115056.htm.

Tschumi, Bernard, Omar Khan, and Dorita Hannah. "Performance/Architecture: An Interview with Bernard Tschumi." *Journal of Architectural Education* 61, no. 4 (2008): 52–58.

Van der Meer, Hans. *European Fields: The Landscape of Lower League Football*. London: SteidlMack, 2006.

Van der Meer, Hans. "European Fields: The Landscape of Lower League Football." In *Landscapes for Sport*, edited by Sonja Dümpelmann, 161–178. Washington, DC: Dumbarton Oaks, 2022.

Vere, Bernard. *Sport and Modernism in the Visual Arts in Europe*. Manchester, UK: Manchester University Press, 2018.

Vigdor, Neil. "The Houston Astros' Cheating Scandal: Sign-Stealing, Buzzer Intrigue and Tainted Pennants." *New York Times*, July 16, 2020. https://www.nytimes.com/article/astros-cheating.html.

Vrentas, Jenny. "Why Some Olympic Swimmers Think about Math in the Pool." *New York Times*, July 29, 2024. https://www.nytimes.com/2024/07/29/world/olympics-swimming-data-analytics.html.

Wahl, Grant. *Masters of Modern Soccer: How the World's Best Play the Twenty-First-Century Game*. New York: Crown Archetype, 2018.

Walker, James R., and Robert V. Bellamy Jr. *Center Field Shot: A History of Baseball on Television*. Lincoln: University of Nebraska Press, 2008.

Wethered, H. N., and T. Simpson. *The Architectural Side of Golf*. London: Longmans, Green, and Co., 1929.

Whannel, Garry. *Fields in Vision: Television Sports and Cultural Transformation*. London: Routledge, 1992.

Whiting, Robert. *You Gotta Have Wa*. 2nd rev. ed. New York: Vintage Books, 2009.

Will, George F. *Men at Work: The Craft of Baseball*. New York: Harper, 1991.

Wilson, Jeff. *Home Field: Texas High School Football Stadiums from Alice to Zephyr*. Austin: University of Texas Press, 2010.

Wilson, Jonathan. *Inverting the Pyramid: A History of Football Tactics*. London: Orion, 2008.

Winner, David. *Brilliant Orange: The Neurotic Genius of Dutch Soccer*. Woodstock, NY: Overlook Press, 2002.

Winter, Tex. "The Triangle Offense." *FIBA Assist Magazine*, July/August 2007, 8–22. http://www.kosarkarski-trenerji.com/ftp/fiba/a27.pdf.

Wood, Jason, and Neville Gabie. "The Football Ground and Visual Culture: Recapturing Place, Memory and Meaning at Ayresome Park." *International Journal of the History of Sport* 28, no. 8–9 (2011): 1186–1202. https://doi.org/10.1080/09523367.2011.567771.

Woodbine, Onaje X. O. *Black Gods of the Asphalt: Religion, Hip-Hop, and Street Basketball*. New York: Columbia University Press, 2016.

World Squash Federation. *Specifications for Squash Courts*. Hastings, UK: World Squash Federation, 2013.

Zillgitt, Jeff. "Things We'd Change in Sports: Expand the NBA Court to Accommodate Bigger, Faster Players." *USA Today*, March 9, 2019. https://www.usatoday.com/story/sports/nba/columnist/jeff-zillgitt/2019/03/09/expand-nba-court-improve-flow/3070024002/.

Zug, James. *Squash: A History of the Game*. New York: Scribner, 2003.

# INDEX

Note: Page numbers in italics indicate figures.


Abdul-Jabbar, Kareem, 122
Aceti, Joe, 57–58
Adler, Dave, 18
aesthetic engagement, 13, 78–79, 96–99; rhythm and, 135; spectators and, 99–102. *See also* grace
aesthetics: architecture and, 96, 98–99; beauty and, 96; grace and, 63, 102; sports and, 96; utility and, 96, 97. *See also* aesthetic engagement; golf: aesthetics in course design for
Aggerholm, Kenneth, 95
*agon* (struggle), 100
Allianz Arena (Munich), 40–41
All-22 Coaches Film (NFL), 58
Ameel, Lieven, 124
*The Anatomy of a Golf Course* (Doak), 44
Angell, Roger, 23–24, 100–101
Anolik, Mark, 130
*Architectural Side of Golf* (Wethered and Simpson), 40
architecture: aesthetics and, 96, 98–99; complexity of sports and, 2, 11; daydreams and, 53; embodied responses to, 4–5; frames and, 3, 27; golf and, 40; perception and, 99; player positioning as, 3, 82–83; sound and, 73; spatial concepts in, 4–5, 8–9, 73, 108; task of, 99; Total Football and, 107–108
*The Architecture of Humanism* (Scott), 4
*arête* (excellence), 100
*Art and Engagement* (Berleant), 98
*Art and Experience* (Dewey), 97
Ashton A's (baseball team), 18–19
augmented reality, 69–70; interpretative data and, 70; point of view in, 70; television broadcasts and, 70–73, 74
Ayresome Park (Middlesbrough, UK), 110–111, *110*

Bachelard, Gaston, 53
Bale, John, 20, 115
ballpark (baseball), connotations of, 116–117
Barber, Tiki, 66
baseball: aesthetic experience of spectators in, 100–102; base running direction in, 144n23; box scores and, 48–49; cultural associations with, 21, 115–116, 154n21; duration of games in, 2; gender and, 117–118; groundskeeper gamesmanship in, 22–23; infield diamonds as frames in, 21–22, 143n11; outfield layouts as frames in, 23; outfield obstacles in, 24; radio broadcasts of, 49, 51–52; sign stealing in, 67–68; spatial perception in, 26; stadium types for, 23–24; strike zone as a frame in, 24–27, *25*; television broadcasts of, 54–57, *56*, 70; virtual strike zone in, 26, 71; women playing, 118
basketball: basket height for, 34,

35; cagers (term for players) in, 36; court dimensions for, 34–35, 38; exclusionary practices in, 122–123; first professional game of, 34–35; free-throw lane (key) in, 36–37; lived religion and, 125–126; Mikan rule in, 37; Naismith's invention of, 34; nets enclosing courts for, 36; phenomenology and, 93, 97–98; shooting patterns in, 90; shot accuracy in, 150n21; slam dunk controversy in, 122–123; social space in, 125–126; spatial perception in, 93; streetball tournaments (Boston) for, 93, 125–126; tactics in, 89–91, 150n19; three-point line in, 37–38, 89–91, *89*
Beckham, Odell, Jr., 61–63, *62*
Beers, William George, 20, 119–121. *See also* lacrosse
Bellamy, Robert, Jr., 55
Berleant, Arnold, 4, 79, 98–99
Best, David, 63, 151n35
*The Birth of Tragedy* (Nietzsche), 100
*Black Gods of the Asphalt* (Woodbine), 93, 95
*The Blade Drive* (podcast), 133
"Body Movement," (Yudell), 5
Borden, Iain, 68–69, 103–104, 124
box scores (baseball), 48–49
*Brilliant Orange* (Winner), 107
Brohm, Jean-Marie, 118
*Bull Durham* (film), 14, 52
Burgener, Pat, 135, 136
Burke, Sarah, 136

*calcio storico Fiorentina*, 115
Camp, Walter, 29
canoe slalom, 20
Carpenter, Jeremy, 133
Carr, Brandon, 62–63, *62*
*Center Field Shot* (Walker; Bellamy Jr.), 55
Centraal Beheer insurance company building (Apeldoorn, Netherlands), 108
Chadwick, Harry, 48–49
Chamberlain, Wilt, 36, 37
Chapman, Herbert, 149n14
Charline McCombs Field (Austin, Texas), 117
Chicago Bulls (NBA), 90
Chillida, Eduardo, 6, 7
*The City of To-morrow and Its Planning* (Le Corbusier), 8–9, *9*
Clark, Caitlin, 91
Clark, Kelly, 136
Clark Field (Austin, Texas), 24
Colás, Yago, 122
CopenHill (Copenhagen), 9–10, *10*
Cordner, Christopher, 102–103
Coyle, Harry, 55–57
Crenshaw, Ben, 41
cricket, 72, 115
Crouse, Karen, 65–66
Cruyff, Johan, 107, 108
Cruyff turn (soccer), 107, 108
Csikszentmihalyi, Mihaly, 66, 93
Cunningham, Merce, 135
Cypress Point Club (Pebble Beach, California), 41, 44; routing of holes at, 44; 16th hole at, 42–43, *43*

*Damn Yankees* (musical), 10
dance: grace and, 103; "presentational realm" in, 79; spatial perception in, 4; as a spatial practice, 3; sports portrayed in, 10–11. *See also* Cunningham, Merce
"Dance Is a Man's Sport, Too" (Tharp), 10–11
Dant, Tim, 59, 63
daydreams, 53. *See also* aesthetic engagement
Dewey, John, 97
Doak, Tom, 44

*dohyō* (sumo ring), 112, *113*; configuration of, 112–113; as frame, 112; purification rituals for, 77, 112; roof treatments of, 113–114
Dye, Pete, 42

Elcombe, Tim, 97–98
*Elogio del Horizonte* (Chillida), 7, *7*
Erin Hills golf course (Erin, Wisconsin), 39, *40*
everyday aesthetics, 96–97

Fallingwater (Mill Run, Pennsylvania), 73
Fan Controlled Football League, 148n40
feints, 94–96
fencing, 5, 19, *19*
Fenway Park (Boston), 23
Feuer, Jane, 61
*Field of Dreams* (film), 17, 117
*Fields in Vision* (Whannel), 58
figure skating: combined skating game in, 80–81, *81*; compulsory/school figures for, 81–82, 149n9; magic circle and, 82; television and, 57–58
flow state (psychology), 93
football (American): downs and distance rules for, 29; flying wedge in, 86, *86*; gridiron field markings for, 29–30, *30*; line of scrimmage as frame in, 29; measurements in, 29, 30; Mesh play for, 87–88; passing in, 86–87; radio broadcasts of, 50, 51; spatial perception in, 88; tactics in, 85–88; television replays of, 60, 61–63; tempo in, 88; video displays and, 66–67; virtual first-down line in, 70–71
Forbes Field (Pittsburgh), 57, 110
Fosse, Bob, 10
Fukuoka Kokusai Center (Japan), *113*

Gabie, Neville, 109, 110–111
Galeano, Eduardo, 6
Genting Snow Park halfpipe (Zhangjiakou, China), 127, *132*
Gibson, Bob, 25, 26
Goldberger, Paul, 116
Golden State Warriors (NBA), 90
Goldsberry, Kirk, 89–90
golf: aesthetics in course design for, 40, 43–44; as architecture, 40; augmented sound in, 74; authorship of courses for, 39, 40–41; course features for, 39; design of holes for, 39, 42, 44; links courses for, 39; natural settings for, 20, 38–39, 44, 45, 137; origins of, 39; picturesque (aesthetic category) and, 44; puzzles in, 39; sound in television broadcasts of, 74; video review in, 65–66
Gotthoffer, Joel S. (Shikey), 36
grace, 63, 102–104; dance and, 103; skateboarding and, 69, 103–104
Grand Sumo: origins of, 111–114; rituals in, 77, 111, 112; television broadcasts of, 114
gridiron (football field), 30, *30*
Gumbrecht, Hans, 100, 102
Gwynne, S. C., 86, 88

*haka* (Maori dance), 77, *78*
halfpipes (snowboarding): at 1998 Winter Olympics (Nagano), 131; at 2018 Winter Olympics (PyeongChang, *135*; at 2022 Winter Olympics (Beijing), 127, *128*, *132*; construction techniques for, 130–131, 133; design considerations for, 130, 133, 136–137; dimensions of, 130, 132, 136; grooming techniques for, 131; history of, 130; spectators and, 133–134, 136–137; superpipes, 127, 128, 132
Hamilton, Scott, 149n9

Han, Jia, 92
Hanson, Christopher, 61
Hawk-Eye ball tracking system, 72, *72*
Hernández, Javier "Chicharito," 93
Hertzberger, Herman, 107–108
Hirano, Ayumu, 127
Hirano, Kaishu, 127, *128*
Holt, John, 63
*Homo Ludens* (Huizinga), 79
Huizinga, Johan, 79–80. *See also* magic circle
Hulshoff, Barry, 82–83, 108
hurling, 114–115

ideology of liveness (television), 61
Ingels, Bjarke, 10
*Inverting the Pyramid* (Wilson), 84

Josey, Chase, 134
*The Joy of Sports* (Novak), 109

Kahn, Louis, 4
Kim, Chloe, 127, *132*
Kimmel, Keith, 130
Kinsella, W. P., 117
Knausgaard, Karl Ove, 3, 15
Kokugikan (Ryōgoku Kukugikan, Tokyo), 113, *114*
Kōshien Stadium (Kobe, Japan), 109
Krakauer, John, 1, 137
Kretchmar, R. Scott, 2

lacrosse: Anglo-Canadian appropriation of, 119–121; boundary fences for, 20 121; commercial interests and, 121; field dimensions for, 121; Indigenous players and, 119–121, *120*; nationalism and, 119, 121–122; "scientific" play and, 119–121; tactics, 120
Lambeau Field (Green Bay, Wisconsin), 109
Larsen, Signe Højbjerre, 105, 125
Le Corbusier, 8–9, 11
Lefebvre, Henri, 135
Levin, David Michael, 103
Lobanovskyi, Valeriy, 85
Loland, Sigmund, 136
Lyttelton, Alfred, 83

MacKenzie, Alister, 41–45: aesthetic principles of, 43–44; Cypress Point Club course design by, 42–43, *43*, 44; military camouflage and, 44–45
MacLeod, John, 90–91
magic circle, 80; perfection and, 80, 82, 96; performative space and, 138; video games and, 80. *See also* Huizinga, Johan
Malevich, Kazimir, 7–8
Mallgrave, Harry, 5
Manning, Eli, 61–63
Maradona, Diego, 102
Martins, Peter, 10–11
Massachusetts Game (baseball), 21–22
Mastro, Maddie, 135, 136
Mazeroski, Bill, 56–57, 110
mechanically reproduced imagery. *See under* skateboarding
*Men at Work* (Will), 22
Mercer, Bill, 52
Merleau-Ponty, Maurice, 94
Mesh play (football), 87–88, *87*
Miah, Andy, 69, 70, 75
Michels, Rinus, 85, 107
Mikan, George, 37
Minute Maid Park (Houston), 24
Monaghan, Paul, 33
Moreira, Zezé, 85
Mullen, Lawrence, 57
Mumford, Stephen D., 152n50
Mumme, Hal, 86–88
muscle memory, 5, 82, 92, 95
Muscular Christianity, 121

Naismuth, James, 34, 35
Nelson, Lindsey, 60

Neuer, Manuel, 91
neuroscience, 92. *See also* proprioception
Nietzsche, Friedrich, 100
Novak, Michael, 99, 109

officiating: automation in, 71–72; measurement techniques for, 30; sound and, 74; video assistant referees (soccer VAR) for, 65. *See also* video displays in stadiums; video review
ollie (skateboarding trick), 103
Olsson, Jan, 107
Oriole Park at Camden Yards (Baltimore), 24

*Painterly Realism of a Football Player* (Malevich), 7–8, *8*
Pallasmaa, Juhani, 73
parkour: embodiment and, 125; settings for, 34, 104–105, 124, 125, 137
"parkour eyes," 104
Pennington, Bill, 65–66
*The Perfect Pass* (Gwynne), 86
*The Performance Cortex* (Schonbrun), 92
phenomenology, 93–94; basketball and, 97–98; embodiment and, 94, 96, 97; feints and, 94–96; snowboarding and, 136; spatial perception and, 94–96
Pipe Dragon (halfpipe groomer), 131, 133
place (experiential concept), 13, 82, 109, 125, 130
*Play-by-Play* (Mercer), 52
playing fields: as architecture, 12; challenges to conventions of, 13–14, 123–125; cultural associations with, 109, 112, 113, 114–117; diversity of, 2, 15; as frames, 2–3, 12, 15, 19; as laboratories of spatial invention, 12, 78; landscape context of, 13, 38–39, 45, 124, 137; mastery of, 98, 104–105; memorialization of, 109–111; memory and, 99; orientation of, 19–20; place and, 109; ritual and, 109, 112; standardization of, 20, 23, 28, 33, 121, 131–132; trial and error in building, 31–32, 130–131; vernacular buildings and landscapes and, 16–19
pleasure points (television), 59, 60, 63
*The Poetics of Space* (Bachelard), 53
Poppen, Sherman, 129
proprioception, 92, 93, 98
psychology. *See* flow state
*Puckelboll* (art installation, Ström), 123–124, *123*

radio broadcasts: daydreams and, 53; first live sports coverage in, 49–50; listeners' connection to, 50–51, 53; listeners' plan (soccer) for, 50, *51*; memory and, 51, 53; studio simulations of games in, 51–53
Rappan, Karl, 85
Reese, Pee Wee, 56, *56*
Retzlaff, George, 60
Richards, Todd, 133
ritual: Huizinga and, 79; in opening/closing games, 77, 80, 112; play and, 79; radio broadcasts and, 51; stadiums and, 109. *See also* Grand Sumo
Robinson, Jackie, 55–56, *56*

Schonbrun, Zach, 92
Scott, Geoffrey, 4
*Shoeless Joe* (Kinsella), 117
Shore, Bradd, 116
Simpson, T., 40
Sims, Tom, 129, 130
skateboarding: embodiment and, 68–69; grace and, 69,

103–104; identity formation in, 69; mechanically reproduced imagery and, 68–69; settings for, 104, 124; style in, 69

*Skateboarding, Space and the City* (Borden), 68

snowboarding: at 2022 Winter Olympics, 127, *128*, *132*; aesthetic engagement and, 135–136; appeal to surfers and skateboarders of, 129; institutionalization of, 129, 131; modified halfpipe event in, 137; origins of, 128–129; phenomenology and, 136; rhythm and, 135–136; risks for athletes in, 132–133, 136; self-expression in, 134–135; television and, 134; tricks created for, 134, *135*. *See also* halfpipes

Snowboard World Championships (1983–1987), 130

Snurfer (snowboarding), 129

soccer: as architecture, 82–83; Cruyff turn, 107; cultural associations of Dutch, 108; duration of games in, 2; goalkeepers in, 6, 7, 91; institutionalization of, 28; *Laws of the Game* for, 28; layout of pitch for, 19–20, 28–29; listeners' plan for, 50, *51*; phenomenology and, 94; radio broadcasts of, 50; sound in, 74; spatial perception in, 85, 93, 108; tactics in, 29, 83–86, 107, 108, 149n14; television broadcasts of, 54; Total Football tactics in, 107–108; video assistant referees (VAR) in, 65. *See also* World Cup

social space in sport, 12, 13, 14, 15, 77, 78, 79, 80, 125–126

softball: field dimensions, 118; gender and, 117, 118; origins of, 118

sound: absence of, 72–73; architecture and, 73; broadcasters and, 52, 74; officiating and, 74; spatial perception and, 73, 74; stadiums and, 72–73, 74

spatial perception. *See under* baseball; basketball; dance; football; phenomenology; soccer; sound; television broadcasts; video displays in stadiums

spatial performance, disciplines studying, 92–93

*Specifications for Squash Courts* (World Squash Federation), 31

spectatorship: Apollonian mode of, 100–101; Dionysian mode of, 100, 101; empathy and, 102; grace and, 102–103; mediated experience of, 12, 47, 101–102; spectrum of, 100, 152n50

*Sport 2.0* (Miah), 69

sports: attractions of, 1, 2, 3, 11, 80, 100; dance and, 10, 11, 69; lived religion and, 125–126; political and cultural identity in, 107–108, 111, 114–116, 121; premises of, 2–3, 38–39, 107; "right way" of play in, 119, 121, 122; risk in, 136. *See also* ritual; social space in sports

*Sprawlball* (Goldsberry), 90

squash: court construction for, 31, 33; courts as frames for, 33–34; glass courts for, 15, *32*, 33; origins of, 31–32; Professional Squash Association (PSA) 2019 Women's World Championship court (Giza), 15, *16*; standardization of court dimensions, 31, 32–33; tactics for T position in, 34

St. Andrews Old Course (Scotland), 39

Stengel, Casey, 25

St. Peter's Park (Ashton, Wisconsin), 17–19, *18*

Stadler, Craig, 66
Stichweh, Rollie, 60
Ström, Johan Ferner, 123–124
*Structure of Behavior* (Merleau-Ponty), 94
Suits, Bernard, 2, 15
*The Summer Game* (Angell), 100–101
sumo. *See* Grand Sumo
superpipes. *See under* halfpipes
Swann, Lynn, 10–11
swimming, 98

tactics. *See under* basketball; football; lacrosse; soccer; squash
Tahoe City Pipe (Utah), 130
Tani, Sirpa, 124
Tatsuno, Kingo, 113
television broadcasts: aesthetic continuum in, 58–59; augmented reality and, 69–73; ballpark dimensions and, 54; camera locations for, 54–55; first live sports coverage in, 54; graphics and data in, 70–72; ideology of liveness in, 61; memory and, 61; pleasure points in, 59, 60, 63; point of view in, 55, 56, 59; replays in, 60–64, 101–102; shot selection in, 55–58; sound in, 72–73, 74; spatial perception in, 55–60, 63. *See also* Grand Sumo; snowboarding
Tharp, Twyla, 10–11
Total Football (soccer), 107–108; Dutch culture and, 108
Tournament Players Club at Sawgrass (Ponte Vedra Beach, Florida): 17th hole, 42
*traceurs*. See parkour
*The Trophy Room* (Gabie), 110–111
Tschumi, Bernard, 4
UFCU Disch-Falk Field (Austin, Texas), 117
uneven parallel bars (gymnastics), 20

Van der Meer, Hans, 109
Verna, Tony, 60
Vick, Michael, 67
video displays in stadiums (jumbotrons), 64; athletes' use of, 66–67; impact on play of, 67; officiating and, 64, 101; snowboarding and, 134; spatial perception and, 66–67
video review: cricket and, 72; FIFA and, 64–65; game flow and, 65; golf and, 65–66; Hawk-Eye ball tracking and, 72; NFL and, 64; tennis and, 72, 72
*A View to a Kill* (film), 129

Walker, James R., 55
Waugh, Doug, 131
Way, Craig, 51
Wembley Stadium (London), 109
Wethered, H. N., 40
Whannel, Garry, 58–59, 63
White, Shaun, 134, *135*
Will, George, 22
Wilson, Jeff, 109
Wilson, Jonathan, 84, 85
Winner, David, 107–108
Woodbine, Onaje X. O., 93, 95–96, 103, 125–126
Woods, Tiger, 65–66
World Cup (FIFA): 1966, 111; 1974, 107; 1986, 102; 2018, 64
World Series (MLB): 1952, 55–56, 56; 1960, 56–57; 2023, 55

Yankee Stadium (New York), 24
Yudell, Robert J., 5

Zug, James, 31, 33